The Complete Comic and Curious Verse

of

Peter Thorogood

With over Eighty Pen-and-Ink Sketches
by the Author

Published by
The Bramber Press
St. Mary's House
Bramber, West Sussex BN44 3WE
Tel/Fax 01903 816205
E mail: stmaryshouse @ btinternet.com

The Bramber Press

Acknowledgements

The author wishes to thank Tony Ketteman for his unfailing courage and perseverance in preparing the text, Diana Durden, who kindly provided some punning names for the Celebratory Ode, and Roger Linton, Jean Whitaker and Celia Gregory for their endless supply of encouragement.

ISBN   0-9538281-2-3

Copyright © Peter Thorogood 2002

Formatting and computer graphics for the Bramber Press by Tony Ketteman

Printed in Great Britain by Gemini Press
Unit 1 Dolphin Road Industrial Site
Shoreham by Sea
West Sussex BN43 6NZ

Our Printer's Preposterous Preamble

This koob may be red from cuver to kover
or, dip ending on the reeder's taste, saverred hear and ther with relisch

Our Publisher's Irritable Interjection

This is a **VERY BAD** start! Please proceed with Our Author's dedication.

This book is dedicated to the memory of
John Bishop
Publisher, poet and friend

Our Author's Irritating Intervention

And don't forget to thank my erstwhile Kensington Bank Manager, Mr. D. Tinkler, whose name certainly has a ring to it. He had a resounding effect on my 'withdrawal' symptoms!

Our Publisher's Ticklish Foot-note

Right! Now we've got over the serious bit, let's get on with Our Printer's 'Praising [or should I say 'grudging'?] Preface'. We haven't got all day, you know!

Our Printer's ~~Praising~~ *Peevish* Preface
by Ivor Grudge

Our Author set out on the lunatic path of comic and curious verse in the early 1950's. A selection of his verse was first unleashed on the unsuspecting members of the Dulwich Poetry Circle by John Stuart Anderson in 1961. Our Author's pen-and-ink sketches were rashly added in 1969 and a small volume, *A Sent-to-Coventry Carol: Verses about Men, Women and Other Beasts*, was published, at great risk to life and limb, by John Bishop for his *Autolycus Press* in 1972. In this new, grossly enlarged edition [if I may say so!] Our Author has brazenly added further hitherto unpublished verses and sketches, together with the original, absolutely ridiculous, but nevertheless utterly genuine, pseudo-critical commentaries, and an authentic laudatory poetical tribute by his Bank Manager of all people! Well, I ask you! Whatever next?

BARCLAYS BANK LIMITED

72 KENSINGTON HIGH STREET, LONDON W8 4SS

5th January 1973

Dear Mr. Thorogood,

> Your book was jolly good,
> Delighting my children, indeed,
> They thumbed through its pages
> For ages and ages
> Whilst making me read and re-read.
>
> I too liked the verses.
> But what makes things worse is
> I cannot stop speaking in Rhymes.
> So to make this craze go, it
> Seemed I should turn poet
> By writing these few awful lines.
>
> Mine lack the perfection
> Of your cute collection
> Any contest – you'd always win it.
> But to turn to your sanction
> (And pardon my scansion!)
> We've marked up a five hundred limit.

P. S. I hope you are not averse to a verse or two.

Yours sincerely,

(Sgnd.)

D. G. Tinkler
<u>Assistant Manager</u>

Inside You Will Discover

9

A Phlatulent Phable!

Synopsis for a Serio-Comic Scenario

Our Author has little to commend himself save for a remorseless compulsion to invent humorous verse. His desperate search for rhymes leads him to spend more and more of his creative hours in his favourite drinking establishments scattered around London. It is clear that he is what the sturdy William Cobbett called a 'university-bred man', a distressing condition that almost sends him to his ruin, and certainly 'mother's ruin'! He lives in a state of deprivation in a basement flat in Chelsea, leased from the iniquitous Bunn family by the widow of Ivor Hunch, the political forecaster, who has come to grief. Our Author's unrequited passion for his landlady only adds to his pathetic state of mind. He finds himself in even more of a pickle than his own 'Upside-Down Man'! But will he succeed in turning himself into a 'Right-Side-Up Man' in the end?

Our Printer, Ivor Grudge, is desperate to get Our Author's book ready for the Christmas trade. He is driven to extremes by Our Author's erratic life-style and his periodic uncontrollable outbursts of 'comic-rhyme disease'. He lives on the top floor of the very same house in which Our Author resides, but, as they have quite separate front doors, they never meet — unless at the Editor's office. In the course of time, he is bound the catch the humour bug and be laid low.

Our (Sole) Reader is the last of his race, since the rest have taken to their beds, suffering from a sore case of 'comic cuts'! He bravely carries on because he has a secret admiration for Our Author's genius.

Our Editors, whose untimely ends are told in a series of *Fatal Fables*, sink helplessly beneath a cloud of comic miasma.

Our Cleaning Lady, Mrs. Rhoda Bristle-Broome, has an extensive family mostly living on the criminal fringe. Her 'bruvver' is fond of playing illegal smuggling games on an international scale. Her 'muvver's bruvver', 'Arfer' Bunn, in the guise of a pastry-cook, is something big in the mafia. As Rhoda is frequently seen riding her broom through the corridors of power, she is referred to by the staff as 'that nosy old witch from Bethnal Green'. She has, however, an abiding admiration for Our Author's genius, and constantly tries to persuade him to write 'serious stuff'!

Our Publisher wisely reigns from a position of complete anonymity. Concerned rather with general policy than the minor peccadilloes perpetrated by Our Author, he nervously steers clear of the 'humour bug' until the final pages, when he suffers from a miserable bout of *la grippe comique*, the deleterious effects of which cause him to cobble a wedding into rhyming couplets for *TheSunday Peep-All*. He maintains, throughout, an insane belief, in common with the Cleaning Lady, that this comic verse lark is really a serious business after all, and that Our Author is some sort of cranky genius in the *genre*.

Peevish Printer's Sore Foot-note

Doo let's get on! I havant gott al day, you kno! My landlady's getting my super erly tenite. She duzn't like to be kopt waiting! What is moor, she puts the lites out at ten and licks the bathroom door to save the hot woughter. I've a hunch she's going to put the wrent up two! I only hope I don't get annuther of my gruggies and call her bluff! The only way round it is to mary the wooman and live wrent phree!
P.S. I haven't had time to poof-read the last paragraff. I can't wait to reed about theranting rhino and the skwirmy 'thing' at the foot of the bed!

Artful Acknowledgements

THE AUTHOR wishes to thank all those contributors who, however readily or dreadily, provided the delirious ditties, ludicrous lampoons, squalid squibs, sore head- and foot-notes, and other passionate post-scripta. He has, however, grave doubts about the flurry of advice notes, sick notes, recovery notes, and other apoplectic apologia; likewise the brainstorms, leg-pulls, afterthoughts and last dying thoughts that pepper these pages. In particular, however, he would like to thank the following:

The Publisher, for his surprising longevity in the face of appalling odds;

Our Publisher's Butcher, for his timely exhortation regarding a nice bit of 'best end'!;

Our Printer, Ivor Grudge, for getting the print the right way round (most of the time!);

Our Printer's Landlady, widow of the political forecaster, Ivor Hunch, for keeping her lodger from coming to a full stop!

Our (Sole) Reader, for his frequently fishy comments (mostly out of plaice!)

Our Cleaning Lady, Mrs. Bristle-Broome, for thoroughly rifling Our Author's drawers and keeping him in a straight line on a very crooked path!

Our Cleaning Lady's 'bruvver' (doing a five-year stretch!) for keeping her supplied with plenty of 'bread'!

Bodger the Bouncer for supplying him with metallic essentials very handy 'inside'!

The Landlords of *The Rover, The Three Brewers, The Five Bells, The Six Bells, The Seven Stars, The Phoenix,* and *The Spread Eagle,* for providing Our Author with encouraging beverages without which this collection of oddities might never have seen the light of day (Our Author rarely did!)

THE PUBLISHER would like to express his undying gratitude to:

Our Animal Psychologist, for timely advice on entertaining rhinoceroses;

Our Anthropologist, for his tactfully worded warning about visiting the Zoo;

Our Cosmetic Surgeon, for advice on looking into mirrors the right way round;

Our Literary Critic, for his comments on Alfred, Lord Tennyson's bunions;

The (Second) Editor, for shedding light on some murky phrases from 'Dorbal' English;
The Zealous Zoo Keeper, for his ingenious analytical annotations on antelopes and alligators;

The **Cambridge Don**, for information about the mysterious case of Professor Grosse-Baer and his 'Early English Anteaters';

Farmer Hodge, for keeping us up-to-date with the neuroses affecting his cow, Lulu- Belle, and ducks, Daisy, Dimple and Emmeline;

The **Cambridgeshire Huntsman**, for providing information about the possible dangers of the pheasant-shooting season;

And last but not least, to the soprano, **Miss Celia Spratpuddle**, who provided a musical note on how to reach the top without really trying!

Appropriate accolades are also deserved by:

The Crewe Cutter, for comments on Our Author's hair-style;

Knitting for Pleasure, with information about irritating nitting problems

The Corporate Hentertainer, with timely suggestions for defumigating henhouses

The Hentomologist, for advice about how to catch fleas;

The Boilermakers' Beano, for proclaiming the genius of Our Author.

We are also grateful to the following for permitting us to make public their amorous adventures and subsequent painful perambulations:

Miss Costa from Aosta   **Ivor Sole-(W)righton** from Brighton

Miss Maureen O'Rourke from Cork   **Miss Grace Auden** from Morden

Miss Myrtle Merrivale from Perivale   **Miss Emily Pugh** from Kew

and Miss Cecily Skinner, who is (quite surprisingly) still living in Pinner.

Waiters!

Nursery Verse

(and worse!)

The Rhinoceros

Who was it chose
The rhinoceros's toes
And those eyes so puny and sad?
      Lumbering
      Clumbering,
In the mud slumbering,
He's oh! such a wily old cad!

One moment he's mellow,
Then he let's out a bellow,
Kicks up such a shindy-din-din;
      Snuffling,
      Scuffling,
He's hopeless at muffling
The clack of his hard, plated skin.

He's oh! so ferocious,
So bumptious, precocious,
His fury is really a farce;
      Snorting,
      Cavorting,
And all that hog-warting,
My dear! On a diet of grass!

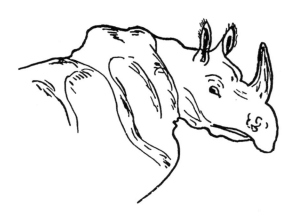

A Social Menace

An Animal Psychologist's View

When inviting a rhinoceros to tea, please be sure that the carpet is of a suitably nutritious quality, as he is quite *a social menace* when displeased. Give him plenty of space as he likes to show his affection by smashing up the furniture. He also enjoys tossing people in the air!

P.S.   He tends to leave rather abruptly by making a large hole in the living-room wall. Do *not* be offended by this. He is more than likely to be paying a surprise visit to the neighbours and has to make a hasty exit.

P.P.S.   It might be just as well to give the neighbours a quick buzz on the telephone in case they are *not* expecting him to call. They will almost certainly wish to make a few preparations!

P.P.P.S.   He specially likes a few sandbags piled up in front of the doors and windows so that he can give then a good old butt on arrival.

P.S. to the P.P.P.S.   The sandbags, not the neighbours!

P.P.S. to the P.P.P.S.   On second thoughts, I think he *would* enjoy butting the neighbours more!

P.P.P.P.S.   Don't forget he's a fast-mover!

P.P.P.P.S. If you live to tell the tale, try adding a P.P.P.P.P.P.S. and, if you really must, a P.P.P.P.P.P.P.S.

A Boisterous Companion

The Tortoise and the Turtle

On 150th anniversary of the birth of Edward Lear (1962), with apologies to Mr. Carroll (aged 124)

Clickety-clickety

O what a trickety

Young tortoise crawled down to the sea!

There he met a young turtle

And in a square circle.

He lumbered around her in glee!

He gazed on her scaly face,

Nearly rolled on his carapace!

He asked her to dine and to sup;

And she cried: "How delicious!

We'll have – how auspicious! –

Turtle soup from a tortoise-shell cup!"

A Nutty Nibbler!

If

What would the animals in the ark have done
If Noah had fallen overboard?"
"Thanked their lucky stars, my son!
They would have had no overlord!"

Author's Wet Foot-note

I thought up these poems in my landlady's bath! I fell asleep. The water overflowed and flooded the whole house. The budgerigar was soused! The garden was awash. All the caterpillars, slugs, greenfly and woodlice were drowned! The dog got a good ducking, the cat came up caterwauling, and I was soaked to the skin. But then, I was the one in the bath. And, as if all that wasn't enough, the landlady nearly gave me the push!

Hydrophobia

on being locked out all night by my landlady!

My budgie's in bed with a *ter*rible cold;
My cat's in the Canaries; my dog's been sold;
I've got the most awful attack of rheumatics; –
I'm taking up flying instead of aquatics!.

P.S. As ladybirds are 'goodies' and eat up all the greenfly, I haven't mentioned them.
P.P.S. I won't miss all the other creepy-crawlies. Ugh!

The Ladybird

Why do we call it a *lady*bird?
For they're ladies *and* gents, I've heard tell;
It seems such a terribly shady word,
When the male 'bird's a 'lady' as well!

Printer's Sneery Queery

'Lady' only in name, surely! Exactly how *old* is the scribbler of this piece of nonsense?

P.S. Don't tell anyone, but *I* like ladybirds too! Especially the 'lady' ones! But then I've always enjoyed chasing *birds*!

P.P.S. My landlady, widow of Ivor Hunch, the political forecaster, doesn't allow us to carry on 'ornithological' pursuits in our rooms!

Family Row

Please Do Not Feed the Animals!

Kangaroo!
Itchy-coo!
Baby in pocket.

Biscuit crumbs –
Itchy-cums!
Trying to rock it!

A Ticklish Problem

Our (Sole) Reader's Reflection
"Has the printer printed this sketch back-to-front?"

Printer's Riposte

No! D.U.C.Y?

The Wow-wow!

Our (Sole) Reader writes:

Have you heard how the Gibbon (or Wow-wow) got its name?

Publisher's Climb-down

We would rather *not* hear, but we *are* willing to, if you *really* insist.

Our (Sole) Reader writes again:

I insist! Here it is:

A pink-bottomed gibbon

Arranged on a ribbon

A garland of primula petals;

If only he'd sat

On a soft Persian mat,

Instead of those sharp stinging-nettles!

Wow!!?!! WOW!!?!!

Printer's Sneering Snort

If you ask me, the poor fellow has got a touch of the sick humours!

The (First) Editor's Deep Thought

And a nasty outbreak of nettle-rash, I shouldn't wonder! At bottom, he's a very sensitive chap! The (Sole) Reader, I mean, not the Wow-wow! This profound poem is undoubtedly autobiographical – though it could be *socio-critical,* or possibly obscure and *political.*

Our Resident Psychologist's Quirky Queery

If we think of the poet as the wow-wow, and the ribbon as 'Life', then the primula petals are...............? and the stinging nettles are.................? and the message is...................?

The Serpent

Of all the hateful beasties
    I hope I never meet,
The serpent not the least is,
    Because he has no feet!

O he'll make me, yes, he'll will me
    To soon put out the light,
Then he'll slither up and kill me
    With a serpentine delight.

He'll curl up at the bottom
    Of my warm and cuddly bed;
O my toes! I know he'll knot 'em
    Up and bite 'em till they're red!

I think I'll turn the blankets back
    To see if he's in sight;
No, there's nothing – not a trace or track.
    O well! I'll say: 'Goodnight!'

Something at the foot of the bed!

Our Resident Psychologist's Piercing Probe

Did *you* imagine there was something nasty lurking at the foot of *your* bed when *you* were a child?

Printer's Rapid Reply

Yes! A devil with an inky face!

Our Cleaning Lady's Appendix

In my case, it usually turned out to be my 'bruvver' hidin' from the cops! Sometimes it was my poor dead husband keepin' out o' the way o' the tax inspector! He was always double-crossin' his double-entries!

Author's Addled Addendum

I might have a word with Our Printer. He knows a thing or two about nocturnal visitors who turn up unexpectedly at the office, without as much as a by-your-leave!

Picture Poem: A Night Watchman

Printer's Quick Minute

I have no time to reply to silly questions. Please write to me in words of one syllable (or preferably no syllables!), being careful to address your envelope to *yourself* and not to me personally. That way you can be sure of getting an answer.

Mrs. Bristle's Brisk Brush-off

I wouldn't even bother, if I was you! . I've just started the spring-cleaning and closed up the letter-box for a nice bit o' brass-rubbing!

The Ballad

of the

Querulous Quail

The Ballad of the Querulous Quail

or

Two Dozen Rhymes for Sale

A Bird in Plus-Fours

This is the tale
Of the querulous quail
Who flew off in search
Of the true Holy Grail.

He searched over hill
And he searched over dale,
Through the blistering heat,
And the sleet and the gale.

With his six young wives –
A polygamous male –
They at last reached the palace
Of the Bishop of Sale.

The Bishop was pleading
(To no good avail)
With a Lady (in audience)
In a black silken veil.

"Nothing would please me,"
She said with a wail,
"As a goblet of claret
And a succulent quail."

"Sire, the larder's quite empty,"
Cried the cook to Lord Sale;
"There's tripe and there's codfish –
And some rather limp kale!

"There's cheese, and there's trifle,
And a tankard of ale,
But the cheese is all mouldy,
And the trifle's gone stale!"

Anything to Please!

The Lady looked up
From beneath her black veil,
Her face filled with horror
At the thought of limp kale.

Yelled the Bishop: "I'll sack you!
I'll clap you in gaol,
If you fail to serve up
A plump, juicy quail!"

His mouth opened wide,
Like the cavernous vale
Where Jonah once dwelt
In the ravenous whale.

Ready to Receive!

The cook on his knees
Cried: "Hail, Mary! O Hail!
Send me, please send me
An amorous quail!"

28

He ran to the kitchen,
All trembling and frail,
His face drawn and haggard,
So twisted and pale.

And what should he find there
Perched right on the flail,
But six juicy birdlings,
And a succulent male.

Prepared for the Table

"We heard you cry 'Mary!'
Is't the Virgin so frail?
Perhaps *she* can tell us
The Place of the Grail."

Cried the Cook: "I must blind you,
And souse you in ale,
And then She must find you
Impaled on a nail."

Such was the tale
Of the querulous quail,
Who flew off in search
Of the true Holy Grail.

He had searched over hill,
He had searched over dale,
Through the blistering heat,
And the sleet and the gale.

With his six young wives –
A polygamous male! –
They had chosen to fly
To the Bishop of Sale.

When at last the Cook brought them
To Our Lady of Sale,
She blessed them, and kept them
To place on the Grail.

There's nothing so bitter
As the pain of betrayal;
But such is the love
Of the querulous quail.

Our Publisher's Interference on Primary Sauces!

It may be of interest to readers to know something of the processes of creation that led our benighted Author towards the completion of *The Ballad of the Querulous Quail*. The following extract from a diary was rescued from the Author's drawers, and thus from oblivion, by Mrs. Bristle-Broome, our nosy-parker of a Cleaning Lady. The notes were scribbled, as might be expected, on a crumpled sheet of foolscap, screwed up into a ball and hurled with superhuman force into the darkest recesses of the drawer, demonstrating thus the desperation of this most desperate of men:

Monday 2 am   Have twenty-four rhymes for Sale, but can't fit in:

bale, hale, rail, scale and *retail.*

Tuesday 4.28 am   I did manage the following:

Rhymes for Sale!

Tale and *quail* and *Grail* and *dale,*
And *gale* and *male, avail* and *kale,*
And *wail* and *ale* and *veil* and *stale,*
And *gaol* and *whale* and "*Hail!*" and *frail,*
And *pale* and *flail* and *nail* and *Sale,*
And e'en (at a pinch) a sly '*betrayal*'.

Wednesday at dawn.   I've had to throw out some of my favourite words:

Liquorice, polyglot, scallywag, igloo, walrus,
iguana, treacle, chubby-dubby, dysentery,
balderdash, artichoke, basilisk, Humpty-Dumpty,
crumpet, marmalade, and parsnip.

31

P.S. I am inordinately fond of *igloos* and *treacle*, and am very partial to *walruses* and *marmalade*, but I always try to avoid *liquorice* and *dysentery*!

P.P.S. I certainly keep *well* away from *basilisks* and *parsnips*!

Thursday 5 am I have spent the night rejecting *capers* and *vapours*, *colic* and *frolic*, *spider* and *cider, giggle* and *squiggle, swanky* and *lanky, ruffle* and *snuffle*, and *rabbits* and *habits.*

P.S. Especially the last pair! Or do I mean *pear?*

Single Pairs

Fatal Fable No. 1: A Nasty Crunch for Ivor Hunch!

Our widow, Mrs. *Bristle*, likes to sing at work, and *whistle.* One day she drank a glass of *punch* with handsome, Mr. Ivor *Hunch*, and, after having early *brunch*, they then enjoyed a lengthy *lunch.* The plot began to *thicken*, and the pulse began to *quicken*, when Our Printer, Ivor *Grudge*, who saw through all the *fudge,* discovered a Mrs. Hunch at home, who simply wouldn't *budge*! One day, there came the dreadful *crunch* and gruesome death of Ivor *Hunch.* He was trapped between two sliding *doors*, betwixt the first and second *floors.* Crushed like a slice of juicy *ham*, he was fast reduced to raspberry *jam*! Now poor Dame Bristle feels the *crunch,* and has no tasty lunch to *munch!*

Mourner's Moan

Well! I think it's a crying shame!

Tricky Poems

The Upside-Down Poem

You'll have to turn a somersault
If you want to read me upside down;
I'm sure you're as sweet as pepper and salt!
But I know you'd rather smile than frown!

The Upside-Down Man

Author's Topsy-Turvy Note

I am sorry about this error. Our Printer says he has had a very topsy-turvy sort of day. His budgerigar looped the loop into the frying-pan and came out frittered, his pet tortoise turned turtle and ended up in Australia, and he (Our Printer, that is, not the tortoise!) travelled to work wearing his reversible raincoat with the inside inside-outside and the outside outside-inside! His message to all readers is:

You will experience a vertiginous upturn on the next page!

The Inside-Out Poem

Printer's Distress Signal

"Actually, I had to look in the mirror to read this poem!"

You'll have to turn your inside out
If you want to read me back to front;
It's only a trick to make you squint,
A sort of (kind of) joke or stunt.

Wishful Thinking

A Cosmetic Surgeon's Prognosis

When you looked in the mirror, did you notice that your left eye was on the right and your right ear was on the left? If they were not, *please, PLEASE* see your doctor **IMMEDIATELY!!?!!!**

meoP tnorF ot kcaB ehT

tnorf ot kcab em daer ot evah ll'uoY
no seerga emyhr ym erus eb ot tnaw uoy fI
.laciteop swal dna selur eht llA
!nosaer ym gnisol m'I kniht ll'uoy wonk I tuB

,nosaes is nosaer rof emyhr eht taht wonk I
(!eno elbaresim a si efil s'tsiruomuh ehT)
!no saep dna ,no skeens, no seeb ni tif t'nac tsuj I
.nup roop a kcarc uoy nehw ertsul sti sesol efiL

efirts dna elbuorT

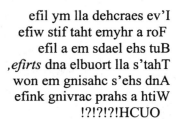

efil ym lla dehcraes ev'I
efiw stif taht emyhr a roF
efil a em sdael ehs tuB
,efirts dna elbuort lla s'tahT
won em gnisahc s'ehs dnA
efink gnivrac prahs a htiW
!?!?!?!HCUO

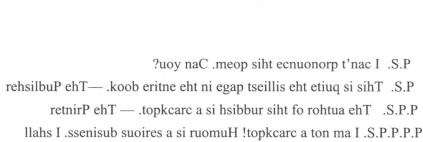

?uoy naC .meop siht ecnuonorp t'nac I .S.P
rehsilbuP ehT— .koob eritne eht ni egap tseillis eht etiuq si sihT .S.P
retnirP ehT — .topkcarc a si hsibbur siht fo rohtua ehT .S.P.P
llahs I .ssenisub suoires a si ruomuH !topkcarc a ton ma I .S.P.P.P.P
eht wom dna nwal tnorf eht tae dna og tsum I ,od I erofeb tuB .tsetorp
rohtuA detnemeD — .edalamram-dna-tsaot

Clue to the Labels

Spoil the French patient to preserve the contents (one word)

Comic Cuts

We have been trying to track down the author of the recently-discovered masterpiece, *meop tnorf ot kcab ehT*, in the hope of obtaining from him a front-to-back version, but he is painfully backward in coming forward. Being a comic versifier, the state of *his mind* may be gravely *maligned*. To say that he's scatty would be truely *unkind*!
P.S. Especially after chasing his *wife* with a sharp carving *knife!*

A Cutting Reply

Printer's Hoity-Toity

The outrageous behaviour of our Author's surly spouse cannot be tolerated. The shocking events described in the pathetic verses entitled, *efirtS dna elbuorT*, published in *The Landlady's Lancet*, are tinged with more than a hint of scandal. We really do not believe our pretentious Humourist ever ventured into a state of matrimony, still less the appalling state of connubial bliss depicted in the *meop*. The scurrilous article is really *deplorable!* Mind you, my landlady's simply *adorable* – but only on *Sunday*, and then only *one day* in six months, I *fear*, in every leap *year!*

Our (Second) Editor's Impulsive Introit

Our (Sole) Reader recommends *Landlady's Tango* and *The Bachelor* for sensational reportage on more of our Author's amorous adventures! It seems that he reveals several skeletons in the cupboard in this sorry story, all in the guise of 'comic verse'! For instance: Who were his mysterious Aunt Dotty and *Friend*? And why did she come to a very bad *end*? The solution we may never discover, of *course*. Our Author is plainly a very dark *horse*!

Fatal Fable No.2: Publisher's Faltering Footnote

Our (First) Editor had a jolly sore *head*, on his way home to his Pimlico *bed*. Confused by the *fuss*, he fell under a *bus*, and a pickpocket swore he was *dead*!

Amazing Numbers

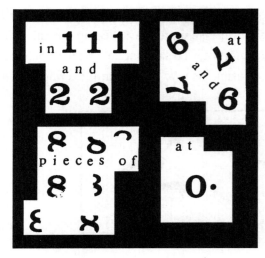

Figures of Speech

Numbers in a Maze

Answers

1. In ones and twos.   At sixes and sevens.   Pieces of eight.   Zero point.
2. Add the numbers vertically, horizontally and diagonally, and what do you discover?

38

The Butterfly

A Metathetical Mystery

"Words, words, words!" – Hamlet

1. The Crime

This is the tale of the slippery path
A small boy follows from bath to bath,
A life full of joys and a life full of woes
Behind the ears and between the toes.

I was living with an aunt of seventy-seven,
In a pretty little house in a village in Devon,
Where time stood still on the cricket green;
I didn't care much about keeping clean –
I slid down the banisters, laid snares on the stairs,
And travelled on buses without paying fares.
I locked up the Vicar and hid in the yews,
I pinched the old ladies from under the pews,
And tickled the Verger with teazles.
I ransacked the pantry and scoffed all the cream,
And tipped the old gardener into the stream.
I tied the cat's tail into several knots,
And painted the dog with bright pink spots
To prove he had caught the measles.

Now, my aunt was a maiden in all but her looks;
Her one consolation was the Bible, and books
Of a ponderous three-volume kind,
Intended for improving and cleansing the mind!
"Now, you, boy!" she sneered, "with your education,
Way, way above your proper station,
Explain to me why – don't stutter! – why
The butterfly's called a butterfly."

She waited and waited for a suitable answer
As I hopped on the spot like a Morris dancer!
"Come, boy, now show your true erudition.
The spell of a witch or a magician
Is not alone responsible for knowledge;
I did not learn *my* wisdom from a college.
Come, now, explain to me the simple fact
Of the origin of the butterfly. Now be exact!"

I thought, thought, thought of a feasible excuse,
Till my nose started twitching and my face went puce,
For I knew she had caught me on the hop,
And once she had started she wouldn't stop, stop
Denying that I knew anything at all,
Except how to climb the orchard wall
In search of Farmer Hodge's pears,
And scrapping about in fox's lairs,
And picking the peas from the early pods,
And teasing the cow with posterior prods,
And using the clothes-prop as a wand
To poke the ducks with on the pond.
She glared at me with her jaundiced eye,
Till she made me feel that to live was to die
A thousand little deaths like the itch-itch-itch
Of the thousand little fleas on the mongrel bitch.

"*Butterfly* derives from *flutterby*, see?
The *flea* was simply exchanged for the *bee*!"

Mortally crushed and immersed in gloom,
I searched through my dictionary in the quiet of my room;
The truth of the matter I longed to lay bare,
But I sought more to punish her for splitting a hair!
The next day at breakfast, I defended my case,
As my aunt nibbled toast with a puritan grace.

Straight-laced

2. *The Defence*

"Distort with your false anagram
The *may* into a sickly *yam*.

There's *more* in *Rome* than *meets* the eye
As the rain *teems* down from the torrid sky.

Keats was a poet and *Skeat* the scholar –
The etymological pundit-wallah!

Willy-nilly, turned about,
Back-to-front or inside out,

The word is a *trap*, so ignore the *part*
Where we talked of the uses of *tar* in *art,*

While I turn my *face* in a *café* or club
To look for a few more *buns* to *snub.*

The *rose* is a *sore* with a fickle *allure,*
Yet the *laurel* is of green as pure as pure.

To *live* is *vile*, as *cold* as a *clod,*
This *life* is a *file* where the *dog* is a *god!*

There's *not* a *ton* but a *mile* of *lime*
To gum the *mug* and *mite* the *time.*

For *did* is *did* and dead as dead;
You can't *deal* the past with a repast of *lead.*

Go twist your letters to an *anagram!*
May *a rag man mash* you for a *sham!*"

3.   The Punishment

Devon, Devon, Glorious Devon,
The land of cream butter, a butter-fat heaven,
Where oodles and oodles of thick rich cream
Soften the lips of a milkmaid's dream,
And puff up the fat of the parson's paunch,
And plumpen the flesh of the young calf's haunch;
Churned into butter to spread on your toast,
Butter to fry with or baste up the roast,

To fatten the piglets and girdle the geese,
And slither the pancakes in panfuls of grease,
To line out your stomach for a night on the tiles,
When you're blotto and plastered and sozzled in smiles.
Through slobbering butter all over his bread,
Man clogs up his arteries, befuddles his head,
And dumps up his torso with dumplings of lead,
With a waistline for miles and miles!

These were my thoughts as I watched her munch
The thick-buttered toast, and heard her crunch
The crisp buttered crust, with a smug expression
That silenced her into a gastric depression.
Yet my pride led me on to develop my theme,
Till I thought my school blazer would split at the seam:

"Butterfly? Flutterby? What a false testament!
The fly takes its name from its butter-like excrement!"

A Flutterby, or, "Come dance with me."

44

Out oozed the yellow fat, greasing her lips.

How she spat on the mat! Gave me the gips!

Her face went as yellow as yellow could be,

Her glance was as black as the cold Black sea,

Her waspish complexion was stung with hurt pride –

But *my* pride was paid with a curdled inside!

Like an ocean-bound vessel alive with the scurvy.

My thoughts turned my stomach all topsy-turvy!

Oh, fickle my fancy to uncover this mystery. –

I'm giving up *English* and taking up *history*!

4. *The Moral*

Never let pride take the uppermost place;

It is sometimes more tactful to yield – and lose face.

When we stand by our principles, the moral is plain:

An eye for an eye is not always humane!

Farmer Hodge's Retort-and-Snort!

I should like to have a word with this' ere young gen'l'man! My cow, Lulu-Belle, is well-nigh *neurotic*, if not downright *psychotic*, and with all that *prodding,* her head keeps *nodding.* As for the *ducks*, well! The *crux* of the matter is *Daisy*'s gone *crazy; Dimple's* gone *simple;* Emmeline's egg-*bound,* has not quacked a *sound* and has gone under*ground.* She'll *never* be *found*!

Local Veterinary Report

We have released the Vicar and untied the cat's tail. We have also scrubbed the dog with paint-solvent and thoroughly fumigated the mongrel bitch. Our Cleaning Lady's gallant attempt to butter up the aunt failed miserably. She refused to melt! And, for what it's *worth*, our Author, in his usual foxy way, has gone to *earth*.

Cleaning Lady's Billet Doux

I still fink Our Awfer's a reelly luv'ly man! He's wrote a be-oo-oo-tiful pome about my sister, Adelaide, which I found in 'is drawers!

P.S. Not the ones with the purple ink *blots*. Not the ones with the plain polka *dots*! Not the lace ones for dancing *gavottes*! Nor even the ones with the gold leopard *spots*! I mean 'is oak chest with the coffee-stain *spots*.

> Adelaide
> Was Granny's maid.
> I do not think
> Her knickers were pink!
> Rather more orange,
> (If I remember).
> I don't think she wore them
> From May to September!

P.S   I *do* like a nice werse now and again, don't you?

Washed out for the Winter Season

Literary Lapses

Six Translations from Dog Latin

Composed by a Roman Centurion in 54 B.C.
Dredged up at Chelsea Reach in May 1959. Thrown back, May 1959!

The inscriptions that follow these masterpieces of primitive Anglo-Latin were discovered by our Cleaning Lady's 'bruvver' when he was caught sinking some loot in the mud at Battersea. They were wrapped in a Roman bikini close to the river site where the verses were discovered. Our Centurion was a trifle illiterate, as his translation of Horace's famous dictum (vide *Canto Tertius*), regarding the usage, and mostly abusage, of 'peeky knees' as a suitable subject for tragic verse, shows.

Cantus Primus: The Goldfish

> Pretty little goldfish!
> Bought him for a bob:*
> Giddy little globe-trotter,
> Glob! Glob! Glob!

Bob = moneta britannicus. "Ante Mercatus Communis moneta britannicus 'multum in parvo' erat!" — *Sterling Notes Vol 2*

The View of a Common-or-Garden Marketeer

"English should be replaced by Dog Latin in all Common Market countries. This would then enable the Latin countries to become *top dogs!*" — *Lingua Franca Clarion*

Cantus Secundus: Split Personality

> Crafty amoeba,
> Living on liquor:
> Divides up its progeny
> Quicker than quicker!

Nota Bene by Nennius, the Ancient Welsh Rabbit

Ipso facto, amoeba astuta non obtusa est!

P. S. Don't forget to warn Our Cleaning Lady!

The (Second!) Editor's Cryptic Correction

For 'bene' read 'bean'. We think Our Author may have done a *runner* and gone a*broad* under the name of *Harry Kott*! Or a man of similar *kidney*! Prior to writing comic verse, he was full of *beans*. Now, he feels a bit of a has-*bean*!

A Social Historian's Snort

Nota Bene: Nennius was never, at any time of his life, a *rabbit*, not by a *hare*'s breadth! And this Roman scribbler is certainly not a ninnius! I tell you what he is, though! He's an utter nincompoopus! Read on:

Cantus Tertius – Sitting Tenant

In my Chelsea room I kept a Pekinese;
It was quite the most uneasy squash and squeeze!
She was far too fat to travel:
Once, she dragged me in the gravel,
And I ended up with two *peeky knees*!

Printer's After-Thought

Or possibly *piqué knees*! I cannot believe centurions rented rooms in Chelsea at that time. Were there *really* Pekinese dogs in Roman London? I *must* ask my landlady when I get home tonight. I have a *hunch* she might just be able to remember!

Cantus Quartus: The Porpuss!

Hungry little porpoise,
Dogged by a catfish,
Fell upon the poor-puss,
Now a rather flat fish!

Horace's Famous Dictum

"Mamma mia! In verses tragico, tings comico not-a so good!"

Translator's Massage

" Plea – sex – cusa my Angle-ish. I learn it now!"

(Sgnd) Giulio Cesare, SPBQ* (retired)

* **S**illy **P**oet's '**B**east-Lover's **Q**uarterly' Award

Publisher's Outcry

This man is a blundering blockhead!!?! Surely, he must mean *paw-puss* — or do you think he could just possibly mean *poo-puss!*

Canto Quintus: The Octopuss!

Coy little octopus,

Delicious with pickles!

Caught in her tentacles,

Death by *ten tickles*!

Verdictum from Virgil's Vet

Watch outibus! De facto, octopus non benignis est!

P.S. Octopuss = *catus octagonalis.*

Catus Octogonalis

Canto Sextus: A Leader of Fashion

My favourite friend is the pachyderm
Who started a cellophane-packet firm;
He escaped like a skunk
With the cash in his trunk
And set up a black-leather-jacket firm!

A Linguistic Loophole

A posteriori, elephantus absurdus est. Coda miniscula ridicula est.

P.S. Pachyderm = *elephantus piccadillyensis* non *wimbledonis.*

P.P.S. I think I'm right in saying the elephant was *trafalgar squaris.*

P.P.P.S. These verses are *so* evocative of social life in Roman London.!

P.P.P.P.S. Just think! They really had cellophane packets even in those days!

Elephantus Trafalgar Squaris

Printer's Knightmare

Last night I had a horrifying dream that these verses were the creation of one of the world's greatest geniuses. He became so famous that his works were translated into every language known to man. Thousands gathered to greet him at airports and railway stations. He was awarded the Nobel Prize for Literature and ended by being appointed Poet Laureate to all the world's leaders. He was literary knight in shining armour.

P.S. I re-read these Centurion verses when I got up this morning only to find they are the most unadulterated tosh I have ever set eyes on. How am I going to get through the day trying to print them? I do believe Our Author has been masquerading as a Roman bard in order to get himself noticed!

P.P.S. Our Author in wit is the greatest *offender!* May we *please, PLEASE* dispense with the witless *addenda*?

A Knightmare

The Great Plague of Our Beknighted Publisher

All our Office Readers now are getting rather *strange*. Like Mrs. Bristle's parrot, they are suffering from the *mange!* In vain, we seek them one by one. We advertise and *search*. No sooner have we found one than the first falls off his *perch*!

Four quartets!

This confused poet left a clue in the toilets!

Comments by Our Distinguished Readers

Winston Churchill: "This is the kind of Inglish up with witch I will not putt!"

Queen Victoria: "We are [definitely] not amused!"

On the Fate of Poetry Popular in its Own Day

The Dame of Shalott
Once suffered a fall,
Whilst playing at tennis
With her racket and ball.
No poet lordlin',
No, not even *maudlin*,
Could save her at all.
The net got entangled,
She was dangled, and mangled
In parts would appal,
Including her bunion –
What a gauche *tennis-onion*!

The Lady of SH!!-a-lott

A Cringing Critic's Carp

This is a perfect example of the appalling whimsicality of our Humourist. A piece of meaningless verbiage. It really makes me cringe. The great Lord Tennyson would be horrified to know that our Author should deign to think of this fine lady of legend as some sort of onion! Even a Tennis-onion!

The (Third!) Editor's Quibble

P.S. Surely, 'bunion' should read 'Bunyan'! Our Printer's error, no doubt!
P.P.S. Perhaps Tennyson suffered with bunions.

A Literary Boffin's Brainstorm
There is certainly no evidence that the Lady of Shalott ever had a bunion!
P.S. Nor even two.
P.P.S. Nor even – sh-sh! – a lot!

The Publisher's Painful Pondering
"I couldn't sleep for the pun about Maud! I hate this poem."

Author's Ratty Retort
I'm so glad you hate it. So do I! Some of my verses are written just so that people can hurl all their hatred of the world at them – so they can screw them up into little balls and throw them at one another. It is thoroughly psycho-therapoetical!
P.S. I'd rather they didn't think of my verses as onions – though, I don't know *why,* the writing of them always makes me *cry*! Poems should really be peeled under *water,* according to a health-and-hygiene *reporter.*

The Cleaning Lady's Brother
This onion-woman must 've 'ad a painful pass-over! I wouldn't mind the mangle if it's going free! Now my bruvver, he's always looking for summink free, he is. He sends me 'is washing home on occasion. There's always notes in his pockets, see? Which I gives to Bodger the Bouncer up *The Rover.* He gives me a loaf to take inside for 'im sometimes. One was so 'eavy I dropped it, and a great big metal file fell out of its middle. I knew it wasn't for 'is front teeth! The little devil!

Publisher's Aching Foot-note
What *is* this woman going on about? I cannot see what on earth our Cleaning lady's 'bruvver' has to do with this Lady of Shalott. *Do* let's get on!
P.S. I can't find 'bruvver' in my dictionary. Is it some sort of rodent?

Fatal Fable No.3
Our (Second) Editor soon came to *grief.* His troubled reign was very *brief!* By authors he was much *maligned.* He sacked them all and then *resigned*! He just had time to say his *prayers,* before he tumbled down the *stairs*! A keen *Observer* of *The Times,* his will was writ in comic *rhymes*!

Fourteen Million Tons of Rain

A Glaswegian Lament

Fowerteen mel-yun tons of rene
Fell last nicht on Glasgie toon!
Sich was the havoc, sich was the panic,
Inshoorance companies shook lack jeely!

'Twasnae the family furniture ruined;
'Twasnae the stench o' the sewers and drenes,
There was but one thung the peeple complened of –
They couldnae get the picture on the telly!

P.S. That fourteen million tons of rain fell on one of Scotland's greatest cities is surely a matter for comment. The Sassenach translator of this original ditty has been threatened with being griddled to a frizzle by a man called Rabbie Burns from Ayrshire:

I tell thee nu, thou'll get thy fairin',
In hell they'll roast thee like a herrin'.

P.P.S. Ms Rene Broadbottom, of Nether Wallop, has written to say that she has been on a grapefruit diet for two weeks and that *Fowerteen Million Tons of Rene* is now an inaccurate description of her weight problem!

Fowerteen Million Tons of Rene

The Man from Ayrshire

The Printer's Dubious Digression

Frankly, this is all about as clear to me as *Beowulf* is to a bee-keeper! As for our Author, he seems to have given up scribbling in favour of the bottle. He has been seen taking more than a pint or two in the *The Three Brewers, The Five Bells,* and *The Seven Stars* all on the same day. It seems that he was carried from Essex Road to New Cross Road to Whitechapel Road on the wings of song, in company with 'the Man from Ayrshire'. Our Author's drinking habits are just about as secret as the Loch Ness Monster! Clearly, a humourist's life is not a happy one — especially the morning after! He was finally rescued from a crowd of cronies outside a pub in Soho , singing home-brewed ditties the vulgarity of which displayed an astonishing degree of originality.

Picture Poem: The Secret of the Lock
Nessiteras Rhombopteryx
or

Answer: Monster Hoax by Sir Peter S

Right, Left and Centre
Poems of a Dissident

Tune: 'Bless 'em all'

1. The Red Rag

Smash 'em all,

Smash 'em all,

We'll bring chaos and strikes to appal;

Abolish promotion,

Create a commotion,

So down with the lot! Smash 'em all!

Picture Poem: Abominable!

2. Band of Choke and Gory

Bash 'em all,

Bash 'em all.

The rich and the proud, make 'em crawl!

We'll get no devotion,

On land or on ocean,

If we don't bash the lot!   Bash 'em all!

3. The Mugwump

"Don't be a mugwump!"
Harold Macmillan: General Election 1959

Chary little mugwump,
Sitting on the fence,
Leans in both directions,
　Has no 'Party Sense'.

Wily little mugwump,
Neither fowl nor fish,
Voting where the wind blows,
　And individual dish!

Right and Left he wavers,
With majority decisions,
Changes horses in midstream,
　Would vote in both Divisions!

Wary little mugwump!
　Politically weak,
Nose among the rumours,
　Too afraid to speak!

Picture Poem: Ragged Robin

Back to Dorbal

A Sogg for Owd Iggladd

Our Scribbler's Thick Head-Dote

"I'b extrebely sorry to addounce that I've fidally sucubbed to bedical beladcholy, add I thidk it will be sub tibe before I ab back to dorbal."

I'b dot dow a Free Bad,

I'b a bed-add-hot-tea-bad,

(Before dawd it is always the darkest!)

By tebperature's soared,

Add the subber is gawd,

I'b depressed by the threat ob the Barxist!

I've a chill od by liver,

I'd like to jubp id the river,

By pulse is all acrobatig;

I'b dib add deurotig;

I'b sick add psychotig,

Add decidedly dubb add rheubatig;

It's so very distressigg,

It's dowdright depressigg,

If the Barxists succeed id the edd;

So I'll get out of bed,

Add I'll banish the Red,

For Owd Iggladd shall be odd the bedd.

Publisher's Bleary Queery

Why are you tormenting us all like this? All I need to have is a *simple* explanation, not a silly one. This alligator business, coupled with the flu epidemic, is driving us all dotty!

Author's Sdeezy Dote

A-chOO-OO!!! I tell you what I deed right dow – an epiderbic! A-A-A-CHOO-OO!!!! Speshly (A-A-A-A!!!) whed I'b busy sdeezigg and sdiffigg (CH-OO-OO!!!!).

Rhybidg Rheubatigz

(by Queed Vigdoria frob her sig bed)

> I'b id bed with the flu,
> So what cad I do?
> By doze iz all Red
> Add by toes iz all Blue.
> I'd give adythigg for
> A spoodful of ligtus
> Add a dice pod of stew,
> But what cad I do?
> Blidkigg flu!

Scribbler's Dote to Tradslator's frob add idto Dorbal Igglish
Key: m = b / n = d / mm - mb = bb / nd = dd / ng = gg

Printer's Hot Potato!
Stay in bed!   Out of my way! My Union is very touchy about this infectious party-political stuff.

The (Fourth!) Editor's Exasperated Explanation
Free Bad = Free Man, or Bodified Dorbal. Appears to imply the condition of the Body being more or less free to do as it likes with but with certain restrictions on its liberty. Barxist = Marxist, or in Bodified Dorbal — Bark-cyst. A disease of the extreme Left side of the Body Politic that ends with the destruction of the Nerve Centre and subsequent paralysis.

Publisher's Feary Queery
I must say I don't like the sound of these Bark-cysts. Do you think we ought to have them treated immediately to quieten them down. They are poisoning the System. The very thought gives me the collywobbles! (See *A Sent-to-Coventry Carol* for an account of the Bark-cyst threat to the Body Politic).

Printer's Passionate Plea
PLEASE let us get on with the next facetious piece of nonsense, otherwise we shall never be able to go to press in time for Christmas! Now, yet another sick note has appeared on my desk!

Fatal Fable No 4: An 'Orrible Obit
Our (Third) Editor died a terrible *death*, gave up the ghost and breathed his last *breath*. He came out in pimples and, frantic with *stress*, he was churned to a pickle and crushed in the *press*. Of his body and soul there remained not a *particle* but was rolled off on Sunday as a full-colour *article*!

The Antelope

I saw a fine antelope
Down by the well,
Sniffing a cantaloupe –
What a foul smell!

Where are you?
I can *bearly* see you!

The Cringing Poetry Critic's View

There may be a whole world of philosophical speculation behind even the silliest of poems, but this is ridiculous! Don't tell anyone, but I'm thinking of going into monastery!

The Alligator

Is this an alligator
In a perambulator,
Eating our Sam?
No more an ambulator,
Sammy's *per alligator*,
Crammed in the pram!

Take-over Bid!

Publisher's Sore Foot-note

Yes, yes! That's all very well, but what about the alligator in the pram? If you want my personal opinion, I think the numskull who thought up these rhymes is as nutty as a fruit-cake. As for the Cringing Critic, he ought to go and take a running sabbatical!

A Zealous Zoo Keeper's Solution

Start by considering the Bark-cyst as the *alligator,* the perambulator as the world of the Free-Bad (i.e. the *ambulator*), *Sam* as 'Uncle Sam' (the ideal world of materialism – that's if you believe in it!), and *pram* as an acronym for 'People Ruled by Armed Maniacs.' Now d'you get the picture? Give me the animals anytime!

P.S. A lecturer from the L.S.E. (Luxury Suites for Executives) has provided our confused Reader with the following explanatory notes to these deceptively simple verses:

Antelope = Anti-Lope(r) i.e. one who is against those who lean too far to the Left or Right, like the Tiny-Totskyites and the Bark-cysts on the one hand, and the Bash'em-All-Up Fronters on the other.

Well = a portmanteau for 'We curse you to hell!' Bark-cyst and Tiny Totskyite jargon for anything that is sweet and lovable to the Free Bad such as "Christbas Puddigg, Bickey Bouse, and the Queed Bother" (though definitely not our Cleaning Lady's 'bruvver'!) He's probably one of them!

Sniffing = the ritual of M. P.'s (and P. M.'s) for detecting a Bark-cyst or a Tiny-totsky even in the geranium bed. It would be more tricky to pick out a little Liberal as their colour is *green* and less easily *seen*.

Cantalope = the 'cant' which the Bark-cysts, the Tiny-totskyites and the Bash-'em-all-Up Fronters use to deceive the Anti-Lopes, as seen in the Party Hymns. The words may be different but they are sung to the same old tune!

A Bark- cyst

A Tiny - Totskyite!

The Cleaning Lady's Second Brush-Off

"It's all the fault of the telly, that's what I say! The Bark-cysts 'ave got control of the BBC (in league with the Tiny-totskyites in charge of Childrens' Programmes).

"Must 'ave a go!" or, A ff-fearsome ff-ff-finale!

There was a young lady called Cecily *Skinner,* who lived in a flat on the outskirts of *Pinner.* She knew a bright lad called Mustafa *Gho,* a seductively charming eastern *beau* (down on his uppers and smart as a *crow*), who changed his name to *Pynchon Reapall* and sent threatening lines to the *Sunday Peep-All.* The lines were not published, and thus were not *read,* and Mustafa's gone 'underground', it is *said.* He works on the District or Bakerloo *Line,* and occasionally is seen on the eight-twenty-*nine!* At night-time he works for a foreign *concern,* with men in dark glasses and money to *burn.* They dwell in dank places, in cellars and *holes,* and barter, for weapons, our lives and our *souls*!

Mrs. Bristle's Intimate Relations

Speakin' of the flu, my muvver's bruvver – not *my* bruvver, but my **muvver's** bruvver – was 'Arfer' Bunn**,** the pastry-baker. He married awf 'is *daughters* to some crooks across the *waters*. They was comfy, all *togevver*, till he was killed awf by the *wevver*!

Picture Poem: One Way Street

Reductio ad Absurdum

Will all readers of those unprecedented masterpieces, *Literary Lapses,* please note that a large parcel, containing over five hundred unpublished comic gems by our relentless Scribbler, has been lost in the post. The matter is, *ergo, sub rosa,* as is the drama of the carving knife related in a previous episode. However, a meeting was held *in camera* to decide on a *modus operandi.* Naturally, the Publisher considers it a *sine qua non* that Our (Sole) Reader should get his *quid pro quo.* Furthermore, this Scribbler has been a victim of *rumpus* in the *campus* and is indisposed. *In vino veritas, et cetera.* His *alter ego* has been severely rumpled. *Nil desperandum!* At present, he is trying to work out a *modus vivendi* for the next few weeks in order to avoid a *post mortem!*

The Ballad
of the
Little Cock Wren

The Ballad of the Little Cock Wren

Branching off, or, Taking a bough!

A little cock wren
Made his autumn abode
With his little wren hen
In a walnut commode!

But she didn't stay long,
This little wren hen,
Ding! Dong! Ding! Dong!
Nor the little cock wren.

Soon they made their nest
In the lush green grass
On the windy west
Where the horses pass!

But he didn't stay long,
This little cock wren,
Ding! Dong! Ding! Dong!
Nor his little wren hen.

So they made their bed
On the tiles instead,
To protect themselves
From overhead!

But they didn't stay long
In a nest that leant,
Ding! Dong! Ding! Dong!
On a sewage vent!

It was very soon after,
In the village church,
They found an oak rafter
On which to perch.

Ding! Dong! Ding! Dong!
Went the matin chimes.
Ding! Dong! Ding! Dong!
A dozen times.

So the little cock wren
Fled the must of decay
(With his little wren hen)
For the flower of the may.

But the blossom had come,
And the blossom had fled,
So how could they know
That the may was dead?

They heard the squawk
Of the hungry daws,
And they gripped the twigs
Hard with their claws.

A sharp wind swept
Through the drooping cloud,
And wrapped the little wrens
In an invisible shroud.

They toppled and fell
On a heap of manure,
In a deathly sleep,
As pure as pure.

But he didn't stay long,
This little cock wren,
Ding! Dong! Ding! Dong!
Nor his little wren hen.

A little girl came
And took them inside,
By a warm log fire;
How she cried and cried!

In an hour, they revived,
And she gave them a bed
And a saucer of milk
In the potting-shed.

Where the horses pass by
On the flinty road,
And the gardener squats
On his old commode.

The Old Commode in the Potting Shed

And he sings this song
Of the little cock wren,
In his home-sweet-home,
With his little wren hen.

Yes, he sings this merry song:
Ding! Dong! Ding! Dong!
Ding! Dong! Ding! Dong!
Ding! Dong! Ding! Dong!
Ding! Dong! Ding! Dong!
But he doesn't stay long!
DING!! DONG!!

Our Cleaning Lady's Yew-lodgy

This Mr. Scribbler is reelly luv'ly, 'e is! I could fall for him any day! He's so 'andsome, and so clever with 'is words. Oh, dearie me! He does love all 'is little animals and birds though! The trouble is, he's not so clever at getting on with the human ones, as far as I can see! Mind you, 'is landlady, widow of Ivor Hunch, got 'is measure with all those birds he used to smuggle in after lights out, and they certainly weren't of the feathered kind, neither! I wish 'e'd write summink reelly *see-ee-rious* for a change.

Author's Agony Grumble

Oh, Mrs. Bristle-Broome! I do! I DO! **I DO!!!** Everything I write is **SEE-EE-REE-USS!** — even the non-sense!

Publisher's Brainstorm the Second

I think this remarkable woman is *right*! We must stem this uncontrollable urge to turn every thing into comic verse and get our Rhymester to give birth to some really **SERIOUS STUFF**. But then, of course, nobody will take him seriously!

Cleaning Lady's Billet Doux

> Dear <u>mister sir</u> gaffer!
> Pleez can we have a pitcher of the poting shed? It's luv'ly. And so are you!
> Rhoda Bristle-Broome

Printer's Enthusiastic Reponse

My dear Mrs. Bristle-Broome, I have the greatest pleasure in enclosing a fine reproduction of the gardener's potting shed. Unfortunately, we had no idea he was sitting on his old commode until after the sketch was printed.

Yrs. Ivor Grudge.

"Home Sweet Home!"

Publisher's Repeat Brainstorm

You know! I do begin to think this remarkable woman is write! Our humourist ought to right more *serious* verse.

The (Fourth!) Editor's Exasperation Extra

Please print 'right' for 'write' and 'write' for 'right'. Otherwise, the meaning is all topsy-turvy, like my head! Do get on! I have to see my doctor in the morning!

Publisher's Retort

Don't interrupt when I'm having one of my brainwaves. Our Author must be encouraged to write *deeply serious* verse. Then we can all stop having knightmares.

Our Printer's Wet Flannel

My landlady has at last unlocked the bathroom. She is having trouble with students who try to smuggle in their girl-friends at night. (See *Landlady's Tango*, written with great feeling by our Author, who seems to know rather too much about the goings-on in our establishment in my view. I must enquire into it.) I am taking her to the Press gathering to meet our Author, so I want to look smart for the occasion. Access to the bathroom would be most acceptable. You never know, we might meet the Lord Mère. (Sorry! there's a misprint somewhere. Anyway, printers have to be squeaky clean these days. Ivor Hunch knew all about that. I'll ask his widow, my respected landlady, Ida Hunch, this evening.)

Picture Poem: Order of the Bath!

Our Manager at the Bank has been suffering from cerebral exhaustion. In normal circumstances he would spend his days sending threatening letters, but he cannot stop himself from making puns. He seems to think he is some sort of fiscal Poet Laureate and now writes all his letters to the bank's clients in verse! Our Author, it seems, has started a banking craze for versifying (mostly worsifying!) which may well spread to the captains of industry and members of Parliament. Before long, Hansard may well be published in blank verse and our letters from the income tax inspector will be composed in rhyming couplets!

Threatening Letters

Elsie:	T, RT?
Arty:	Q, LC!
Waitress:	24T?
German:	VR4T,2!
Waitress:	O, IC! UR24T,2
German:	9! VR44T
Arty:	DUC a Q,A?
German:	O! UQ4T2? VR44T
Arty:	OL!
Elsie:	UR a BF!
German:	UR a BF2!
Arty:	O! go 2L!
German:	OU go 2L2!
Elsie:	OG! I8U!

Silly Verses

Spitting Image

Large-lipped	Shaggy-baggy
Honey-eating	Glibble-dribble
Bear from Ceylon;	Just like a don!

A Cambridge Don's Idle Doodle Discovery

I really *must* object to this offensive portrait of Professor Grosse-Baer of Berne. The photograph of the Professor, in which he is seen wearing plus-fours and smoking a six-foot alpenhorn, fell out of his travelling-case at Dover and is actually a whisky-stained study of an anteater! The Professor, in true Byronic tradition, kept the creature in his college rooms whilst on a British Government Grant for research into the political ideas of our early British Anteaters.

Unfortunately it was not discovered until it was too late to cancel the Professor's visit that the Ministry of Education and Science had unwittingly allowed a typing error to alter the direction of Professor Grosse-Baer's research. Apparently, An_teat_er *should* have read 'An_cesto_r'! The mystery was uncovered in an idle doodle on the wall of his college rooms.

Professor Grosse-Baer and a British Ancestor

Printer's Apologia Pro Suum Migraine

Owing to the inanities of our Author, dubbed 'Scribbler', I am three-quarters indisposed. It is with regret that I shall have to have him sequestrated, painful as it may be to cut him off from his bare essentials!

Scribbler's Beery Queery

Does it hurt? I don't want to lose my marbles!

Printer's Apologia Pro Sua Apologia

Oh really! We mean your typewriter and your favourite tipple. So sorry, old boy!

P.S. I must ask my darling Ida if she has a hunch as to whether there really *was* such an idiot as this Professor Grosse-Baer! Is he just some fanciful *theme*, or a whimsical prank from *Academe?*

Our Cleaning Lady's Chit-Chat

I went on one o' them baggage-tours once, 'cos my bruvver had some fings ter deliver to some bloke in Swizzyland. That's why he's doing time, see? Anyways, there was these great fat bears squattin' in a big hole in the ground, munching bunches o' carrots. There was this one who'd rubbed 'is tummy so 'ard he'd rubbed all 'is fur awf. Cruel, it was! They don't give 'em no bicarb nor nuffink, and I'm as sure as sure he had a right ol' belly-ache! Shouldn't be surprised if it wasn't something to do with this Professor Grouse-an'-Bare geezer. He was 'is spittin' image. As a matter of fact, he might 'ave been the one that spat at me summink awful. I won't be going *there* no more, I can tell you. Anyways, my 'bruvver' had to get 'isself tattooed — secret messages he had to get through the customs about some 'big stuff' he had to collect. I don't know why he gets 'isself mixed up with that Bodger the Bouncer. It must 'ave bin summink to do wiv my muvver's bruvver, 'Arfer' Bunn. He was one of the churly Chelsea *Bunns*. He 'ad two daughters and ten *sons*. One son-in-law made his fortune in *raffia,* and one was summink big in the *mafia*!

Picture Poem: Tattoos!

75

The Ibex

I once saw an ibex
Under an ilex
High on the Apennine range;
His eyes were cross-crissing,
His left horn was missing;
Oh! he really looked *ever* so strange!
Silly old ibex
Under the ilex,
Why do you look so forlorn?
In Alp or in Apennine
There's nothing so asinine
As an ibex with only one horn!

Is there something missing?

The (Sole) Reader's Reservation

After the dubious nature of the investigation into the mysterious *Antelope* and *Alligator* verses, I have my doubts as to the correct interpretation of this *Ibex* effusion. Is it about ....or is it about........?   I don't know.   Maybe it's autobiographical!

I Wonder as I Wonder
or, The Critic's Dilemma

The knack of the thoroughly versatile critic
Is to ask awkward questions and be analytic:

Do you think it's just graphic,
Pindaric or Sapphic,
Is it simply facetious and sad?
A false panegyric,
Satirical, lyric,
Or plain pornographic and bad?

Is it true, analytical,
Or dark and political,
Was it scribbled straight down off the cuff?
Is it laboured or churlish,
Or coy-little-girlish,
Or subtle poetical stuff?

Our (Sole) Reader's Candid Confession

Don't ask me! After all – I'm only a literary *man*. I should ask a devoted admirer or *fan*
It might just be 'dark and political' *stuff*. The meaning's as clear as blind-man's-*buff*!

Our Printer's Political Point

It is possibly a little *conservative* in tone, and rather *laboured*! Even a little *liberal*! At
all events, he's an odd *party*, Our Scribbler.

Mrs. Bristle's Brush-Off

You know what I fink? It's a 'orrible fizzeeshus pawnygraffy! If my 'bruvver' got 'is
'ands on this kind o' stuff he'd make a fortune on the underground. And I don't mean
the Chewb, neither!

The Quetzal

A Waltz

Who is it
Whets all
Our hopes
For a craze?
Who is it
Gets all
Our ration
Of praise?

It's the quetzal,
Dazzling quetzal!

Who is it
Nets all
The cash on
New ways?
Who is it
Gets all
The fashion
Displays?

It's the quetzal,
Dazzling quetzal!

Yes! So let's all
Start a craze!

Publisher's Natural Reservation

Judging from the remarks made by the Zealous Zoo Keeper about Antelopes and Armadillos (or was it Crocodiles and Alligators?), this poem may not start a craze, but it may well set off a revolution! It is so *utterly* trivial it must surely be really **SERIOUS!**.

Fashion Display

Our (Sole) Reader's Queery

What *is* a quetzal anyway? I always thought it was some sort of biscuit!

What is a Quetzal Anyway?

A Serious Reply

The quetzal's tail is three feet (and more!),
Her feathers like long bright streamers,
Spirit of nationhood, spirit of gods,
A beauty undreamed of by dreamers.

This extravagant bird lives in plush Costa Rica,
And the jungles of lush Guatemala;
With her feathers of crimson and brilliant green,
She'd make a good show in your parlour!

Printer's Billet Doux

Now, this is a bird I could really go for! What did you say her name was?

Author's Interjection

The biscuit is a 'pretzel', not a quetzal! Please don't ask me to invent yet *another* rhyme about it!   I mean, if you like, I could start with *bets all* and *debts all* and....!

Printer's Anguished Answer

STOP!! Please. don't go on! You are developing into a sad case of verbal *diorrhoea* of the comical kind.

Our Cleaning Lady's Sniffy Snitch

It's *dire 'ere* sometimes, an' all! Cleaning up this office is a nite-mayor!

Fatal Fable No.5: The Fourth Editor's Frustrated Finale

His life was one long ampersand, a series of dark *terrors*, obsessed by hyphens, commas, dots, and countless writer's *errors*. His bark, as fearsome as his bite, he did not ever *weaken*; his face, when printer's devils played, flashed like an angry *beacon*. He had a bright vermilion nose, resplendent with a *mole on*; alas, his prose a full stop met, with a strangulated *colon*!

The Yak

If I had as much hair as the yak,
I would not be a teacher
Nor even a preacher,
For such a display would look slack;
With my head in a fur suit,
I'd be terribly hirsute,
If I had as much hair as the yak!

If I had as much hair as the yak,
I am sure I'd be given the sack;
The girls would all simper,
My locks would grow limper,
Till I had them trimmed
Front, sides, and back,
If I had as much hair as the yak.

The (Sole) Reader's Curlicue
This is rather a hairy poem, but it grows on you!

A Tibetan Long-Hair

A Cutting Comment!

In our opinion, the author of this hair-piece is prejudiced in favour of the *Crew Cut.* If he is, we would like to give him a sharp clip round the ears and finish him off with a friction! —*The Crewe Cutter* (Xmas Edition)

Population Explosion!

By Rhoda Bristle-Broome

(translated from the original Cockney by Ivor Grudge)

Next door to me in Bethnal *Green*, you've no idea what I have *seen*! A family of twenty have come to *stay*. They chat to their neighbours. They sing all *day*. Their motto seems to be: 'Let's make *hay*'! Next door but one, live Mister and *Missis*, two children, one dog, a cat that *hisses*, while upstairs Granny sits and *moans*, and grumbles about her life, and *groans*, while kindness to folk she *dismisses*. She's obsessed with her parrot! Her life's such a *bore*! She never *once* thinks of the family next *door*!

Population Explosion

Sensible Verses

Press Gang

Our planet's beset by a dangerous plight,
With its nations all grabbing (for wrong or for right),
While cant correspondents spread doom and despondence,
And the media relish in violence and spite.

The world loves to read a sensational press,
A scandal, a plane crash, some marital stress,
A mugging, a murder, a blow on the head,
"Hurricane strikes with hundreds of dead!"

"Oil-tanker aground!" and "North Sea pollution!"
"Middle East peace talks!"-- with no real solution.
"Crime on the increase!" and "Fire on the Ferry!"
"Flooding in India!" "Insurrection in Derry!"

The dearth of compassion one everywhere finds,
Shows the media is set on controlling our minds.
My birthday's tomorrow; there's one present I'd like:
To hear, in the morning, the Press are on strike!

Our Bank Manager's Advice Note

I must show this poem to my daughter, Isabella Tinkler, as it has a certain ring about it!
I'm not averse to this sensible *verse*, but no news of the markets would make things still
worse! Investors would be scared for their prime *stocks and shares*. The news would
bring nothing but sharp *shocks and stares.* Like shepherds who lose all their sheep to the
wolves, they'd be chased by the *bears* and tossed by the *bulls*!

Publisher's Pertinent Protest

Apart from the loss of the nude and *the rude*, how would we get our new book *reviewed*?

Our Cleaning Lady's Clean Sweep

When I've swept up the dust and wiped down the *doors*, and polished the doorknobs and
mopped all the *floors*, a day with no 'dailies' would be all very *well*, but no papers to
walk on would be absolute *hell*!

Split Personality

I'm very like the spry Ducrow,
That famous London circus *beau*,
Who, nightly, before astonished eyes,
Bestrode four horses in a row —
A kind of comic *tour-de-force*,
A man too agile for one horse.
Compared to his, my own conflicting talents –
To paint, compose, write poetry, do research –
On backs of muses strive to keep the balance,
Demand expression, struggle for a perch.

A roll of drums! A shout! "Strike up the band!"
I stand astride my horses, reins in hand.
Four sets at each exhilarating show!
And round the circus-ring of life I go,
My muses galloping and cavorting,
Foaming at the bit, noses snorting,
My talents adjusting to every tilt and lurch –
Now painting, now poetry, now music, now research!
I do it all in comic starts and fits.
I hope, like poor Ducrow, I shall not do the splits!

Jack-of-All-Trades

85

House Mouse

Holland Street, Kensington 1972

At the edge of the carpet
A small brown shadow
Flickered for an instant
And was gone. It was comic!
Was that vodka too atomic?
Perhaps the pâté was too rich.
(The liver plays wicked games
With the innocence of eyes!)
Whatever it was, or might have been,
The edge of the carpet could be seen
To have all the appearance of being —
The edge of the carpet!

A minuscule brown ball of fluff
Hovered for a moment like a tiny puff
Of smoke from a toy electric train.
Then — squeak! squeak!
Hop, skip, and scamper,
Four little feet
Nimbly manoeuvre in balletic style
Enormous palisades of pile.

Clumsily, I — a grim, gigantic ogre —
Clamber over the mountainous sofa,
Maraud the territory,
Like a hideous brontosaurus,
To terrify a prey so frail —
No longer than my thumb
If you include his tail —
Round and plump as a suede button.

Curtain-hangers!

Grasping a saucepan in my hand,
I jump, I leap, I crouch, I stand,
I pounce, I strike! — and limp,
I trap this cowering and yet cheeky imp.

The memory of his mangled corpse
Crushed to a pulp of blood and bone,
Will *not haunt* me
As I free him under the lilac tree,
See him scurry through my neighbour's door,
Whilst I, gaping in the street,
Contemplate my saucepan, emptied now
Of those pattering
Metallic-sounding tiny feet.

Today — he came back!
No attempt to hide!
Up the curtain, across the pelmet,
Down the other side.
Hop, skip, scamper, squeak!
He makes me feel so vexed.
You see, there is no telling
When he will come again
Or *what* he will do next!

Mouse Mesmerism

The Flea-Catcher

Hampstead Heath, London 1973

"They feed on human blood," he said,
Happily rolling up his sleeve.
A pattern of tiny specks of red
The tiny flea began to weave.

"I'd give anything, a pound a dozen,
(The going price in news reportage),
I heard it first-hand from my cousin,
The reason why there's such a shortage:

No self-respecting, upright bloke
Admits to having fleas to spare
Nor lets me peek, and pick, and poke
Among his neatly-managed hair.

I cosset 'em and lead 'em on,
Find their talents, and potential,
For very soon they're dead and gone!
Quickness and lightness are essential.

The harnessing is really tricky.
(Careless is as careless does!);
Fingers must be dry, not sticky;
Be sure to clear away the fuzz.

There is no end to how they play:
Some carry things, without a care,
Some march in lines across their tray,
Some jump and leap and whizz through air;

Some dance and skip in ballet-style,
But anyone who knows a flea
Must surely understand that he,
The flea, whom mostly we revile,

Has time-span of a few short days
In which to learn a life-time's wit,
And study all his trainer's ways
Of teaching him to jump or sit.

The only trick to make 'em stick
Is fresh red blood to feed their feeders.
The secret is to train 'em quick,
For soon, they'll die. Poor little bleeders!

Feet of Agility!

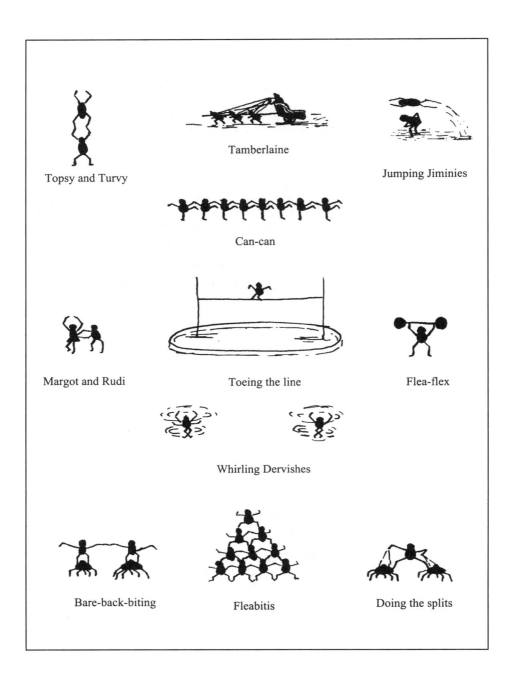

Topsy and Turvy

Tamberlaine

Jumping Jiminies

Can-can

Margot and Rudi

Toeing the line

Flea-flex

Whirling Dervishes

Bare-back-biting

Fleabitis

Doing the splits

The Flea Circus

Horrid Verses

The Animals Conspire Against Adam

In a green shady spot by a fox's lair,
Below pendulous branches of apple and pear,
The viper and vulture and vixen were there,
And greed turned their eyes to stones.

The viper hissed first: "Yes, I'll poison him fresh!"
Screeched the vulture: "I'll mangle and tear at his flesh!"
Scowled the vixen: "I'll tangle his pelf in a mesh,
And weep crocodile tears on his bones!"

A Pychoptherapoetical Diagnostician's View

The Author of this poem, modestly or *shyly*, damply or *drily*, describes himself as a 'Scribbler'. A mouse could not *nibble* more *slyly*, nor *dribble* more *drily* than this game little *poet,* but, then, does he *know* it? He should not be *hounded,* with such talents *unbounded.*   Our age of *anxiety* has no such *propriety* where the animal world is *concerned.* Our author has *learned* to suffer alone, with the threat of his books being *burned*!

Publisher's Protest

Piffle! This psycho-therapoetical person is a raving lunatic!

Printer's Retort

We agree on something at last! He's as potty as a pot-plant!

Press Cuttings

If the 'green shady spot' is in the London area, will the owner please contact us immediately as we have long waiting-list of prospective purchasers. All sitting-tenants will be rehoused. The Chelsea poet with the Pekinese (or peeky knees, whichever still applies) need not get in touch. — *The Social Escapologist.*

These verses are a deplorable example of warped wit at the expense of defenceless animals and should be suppressed. Similarly, all references to human beings as cats, dogs, snakes, rats, pigs, sloths, cows, donkeys, skunks and ferrets (which they invariably are) should be confined to a menagerie. -- *Animal Rites Quarterly.*

More Adverse Adverts

The price of apples is down this week, though the pears are high! In fact, they've paired off and gone off.! — *Barrow-boys' Bulletin*

Peared Off

Any good rounded relationship should be soft and curvy, just like the happy *pear* above. — *Agony Aunt's Advertiser.*

The Worst Unconscious Pun in the World, by Rhoda Bristle-Broome

Noah must 'ave bin a Cockney, 'cos when God called out: " 'ark, Noah!", the old geezer though he had to go and build a flippin' boat and fill it wiv all them 'orrible snakes and crocodiles. Now, if he'd bin a bit more hedgerkated 'e woulda listened proper, and the world would woulda bin a better place, wouldn't it? I ask yer! Some people! Pity the 'ole lot didn't get washed overboard, 'im an' all!

Picture Poem: Life-boat!

The Last Louse

Two hungry woodlice (xyloghagi)
Were sitting among the sarcophagi
Filling their empty oesophagi
    With granity grit from the stone.

The male was for sharing and halving,
Should they chance on a dainty wood-carving;
But *sans* oak or elm he was starving,
    So he munched up his wife to the bone.

Publisher's Caution

This is clearly a case for the Committee for Human rights. No male, louse or otherwise, should be allowed to get away with this sort of thing.

Cleaning Lady's Lunch-Note

I don't *eat* people but I *do* like *m*eating them!

Picture Poem: Exchanging *Vow*(el)*s* for a *Happy* New Year!

A Close Shave

Today I saw a Jaguar,
So silent, sleek and lithe;
It ran right on a zebra
Down near the docks at Hythe.

I watched its red eyes blinking
As it sped into the fog,
And I wept to think it wasn't me
Lay dying, but my dog!

Printer's Post-Prandial Palpitation

This poem gives me the collywobbles. It's the most gruesome case of 'cat eat dog' I have ever come across.

Our (Sole) Reader's Teary Queery

As the (Sole) Reader, I have a right to be warned about poems coming up like this. It is clearly not 'animal', and there's no sense of it being at all 'vegetable', so I suppose it must be 'mineral'! I had better go and ask my driving instructor! He knows all about Jaguars.

Printer's Condolence Clip

The bereaved Author must have loved his dog very much. I wonder if it was a Peeky-knees!

Author's Sore Leg-Pull

Of course, he was Pekinese. Or, perhaps you think he was Portuguese, Japanese or Double Dutch! Or why not Double Gloucester! Really!

P.S. Which reminds me! Talking of Gloucester, there was once a mysterious Miss *Costa*, who went on a cruise and they *lost her*. She came back quite *old*, with a fortune in *gold*, and nobody knew what it *cost* her!

P.P.S. Now I think of it, I'm sure I've heard a verse like that before! I must ask Doctor Foucester. He ought to know what it coucester. I believe she lived in Aosta!

Lines to an Astronaut

Do not take water to the moon
Beneath the dust the rock is porous.
Who can tell what hideous things
Old H_2O could spread before us.

Things that follow in our traces,
Poisonous, sluggish grey balloons,
With sticky feet and oozing faces –
Even H. G. Wells would swoon!

Please don't take water to the moon,
However spacemen may deplore us;
We might discover all too soon
Another deadly dynosaurus!

From Our Resident Astronomer

Moon-rock is definitely not *porous*. Nor for that matter is a dino*saurus*.

Publisher's Piffling Protest

I *have* heard of 'the waters *of* the moon' but is not the concept of water *on* the moon all the stuff of fools? I *do* wish our Author would get his facts right on these points. Which makes me think! Perhaps I ought to get in touch with our Literary Agent, Ivor Sole-*Wrighton*, from somewhere near *Brighton*, whose teeth he was unable to *bite on*; he swallowed some *goat,* and it stuck in his *throat;* now he would be an absolutely fascinating person to *write on*! Or even *alight on*!

Our Author's Painful Complaint

I have, with this silly *gent*, been resolutely dili*gent*
And stuck close to the *forces* of primary *sauces*!

Loathsome Litany

From phantoms and phonies
And out-of-tune fiddles,
And small tufts of hair in the jam,
From mealy-mouthed moanies
And maddening riddles,
And worms that crawl out of the ham!

From loud belly rumbles
And gristle-boned beef
And hunger and thirst on the dole,
From grizzles and grumbles
And poor man's grief,
And blindness as blind as the mole;

From puking and spewing
And odours and scum
And insidious growths of the body,
From chewing-gum chewing
And mould on the crumb
And things that are tawdry and shoddy;

From vampires and leeches
And flea-bitten bats
And Crippens that crouch for a crime,
From pestilent creatures
Like termites and rats
And things that crawl out of the slime:

Good Lord, deliver us!

Nurse Penny Sillin's Blunt Point
I don't wish to needle you, but what's the point of this poem? A quick jab in the backside can purge you of these phobias. Bend over!

Publisher's Pointed Protest: Oo-ouch-ch!?!?! Don't do that again!

Three Fellow-Travellers

1. Sleeping Partner

How I loathe the pestilential little nit!
Paralytic, parasitic, without wit;
It's so peaceful when he's egg-bound,
O, but when he's nipped my leg round,
I'm not sure if I can stand or sit.

Scribbler's Scratchy Scrawl

I can't for the life of me remember whether this little fellow was an English nit, a French nit, a Bulgarian nit, a Greek nit or just a plain nit   At all events, they are great little travelling companions! Once they adopt you as their host, they're so loyal they'll stick to you forever!

2. The Liver Fluke

Nasty distomium,
Lily-livered worm!
Needs no encomium
To make a man squirm!

En-comb-ium

Press Cuttings

Why not enjoy a good knit! Back numbers still available for patterns in bright colours. Sure to bring out the best in you! — *Knitting for Pleasure (Pins and Needles issue)*
Let *us* clean out you chicken-house! Don't put up with fleas.   Let *us* do all the head-scratching for you. Your hens will simply love our fumigation methods. They will assuredly get their feathers well and truly ruffled.. — *The Hentomologist. Vol 13*

3. A Ticklish Dilemma

We received the following *nit*ty ditty from a Cambridgeshire gentleman who is clearly *itching* to give your very own shooting-party the benefit of his experience:

> Today is 'The Glorious Twelfth' so proud,
> When pheasants begin to look *sheep*ish and *cow*ed!
> So beware you young farmers, when crouching in reeds,
> You don't catch a tick in your gaiters and tweeds!
> It's so very nasty to dig with a pin
> For a sly little tick tucked up in bed in your skin!
> Avoid at all costs those sheep-ticky places,
> For ticks have strong jaws – and peculiar faces!

Press Cutting

Living on tick? Get the *most* out of your *host*?— *The Corporate Hentertainer*

Publisher's Rumble, Mumble and Grumble

This Scribbler has succeeded at last! He has turned me into a human wreck!
My inside is going up and down like a yo-yo. My head is on a see-saw!

Publisher's Second Tummy Rumble

This man is not only an ass, he is a double ass. Please! PLEASE!! Be good enough to
ass-ass-inate him immediately.

Ass-ass-ination

P.S. For this *prank*, I must be *frank*, I have to *thank* old George Cruik*shank*!

"Hallo! Are you there? Is that Mrs Bristle? Can you hear me? It's a wonky line! I have got the most incredible hunch! No, not *lunch*, -- <u>hunch</u>! Look, can't you hear me? Yes, hunch! What? Oh, I know old Hunch is dead and gone. No! I mean 'thought', 'suspicion'! – you know! Look! It was like this. I was having a drink in *The Seven Stars* in Strawberry Hill, see? No, not Norbury -- <u>Strawberry</u>! Anyway, I suddenly saw all these enormous balloons -- No, no! *balloons*! Not <u>bassoons</u>! -- with sticky feet and oozing faces, see? I know it's customary to see pink elephants, but I saw balloons. I think it was the double vodka! Then I thought, wouldn't it be weird to escape to the moon and see it for myself. In a flash, I realised that it was my erstwhile friend, Madam Hunch, looming up through an alcoholic miasma. What? No. no! woman! Not *my asthma* -- <u>miasma</u>. And what's more, she was on the arm of Our Printer, Ivor -- wait a minute! Who is that speaking? Why, it's you, Grudge! Now, look here! What's going on? I'm supposed to be talking to Mrs. Bristle. Look here! If your taking a shine to Ida Hunch I shall want to know why. I shall talk to Our (Sole) Reader. He always knows anything fishy that's lurking about, and – he can smell a rat a mile off!

Picture Poem: Strawberry Hill

Printer's Ruthless Recommendation

This crass ass ought to be sent to a head-shrinker. I shall have to keep clear of this fellow. I've a hunch I shall pass him on the stairs one of these days! I hope he won't bear a grudge! Even a small one.

Publisher's Gammy Foot-note

As he's such a fat-head, it should improve his appearance enormously!

Wicked Verses

Tales of Innocence and Experience

1. The Child I Rue So!

When I was a boy, I had many a toy, but I really loved most my Robinson Crusoe;
Though much did annoy, I remember with joy the tale which I grew so and knew so!
On our wall was a print, I don't think by De Wint, and I'd buy it if yet I could do so,
Oh! It would not annoy to live like that boy, with 'Good Friday' and funny old Crusoe.

Picture Poem: Old Prints

2. The Rake's Progress

How very appealing, and extremely revealing, to see his dark secrets unfold!
They're there on the ceiling, inscribed with such feeling, how he came to be out in the cold.
He drew with a paint-brush, what was viewed with a faint hush, a life full of lust and of gold;
Full of wheeling and dealing, though not really stealing, the facts of his life were unrolled.
Now his heart is congealing, from too much concealing (more than ever could really be told).
He's recovered with healing, repented with feeling, and no longer bold –   now he's old!

Two Gloomericks

Man

Man is a mammal,
But then so is a camel,
A mouse, or a cat, or a mole.
The only distinction?
Man's doomed to extinction
If he favours an atomised soul!

Gentleman's Agreement

Woman

When Eve plucked the apple
For her young man to grapple,
God spake a few words off the cuff:
"My Eve, you're so pretty,
But, oh! What a pity
Adam wasn't adamant enough!

Body Beautiful

Slithery Tails
Jungle Story

Of Aunt Dotty's close friend, a *rotten lot*, I have really, I'm sorry, *forgotten what*, he did or he said to *beguile* her, and eventually to spite and *revile* her. Aunty suffered a terrible *breakdown*, and went out to see him in *Capetown*. He came back from the *jungle* with a mysterious *bundle* that wriggled and waggled and *hissed*, but gifts she could never *resist*. The story appeared in the news, it was *said*, how he came to be rich and she came to be *dead*! I found all about it in the Capetown *Rag*. He was captured and 'courted' for his share of the *swag*!

A Snake in the Grass

Snake Snack

Dusting her baubles,
Aunt Dotty, she warbles
A ballad or two.
Coiled in her bric-à-brac,
Snake! Snack-a-snick-a-snack!
Mind, Aunty! Oogh!
On his expensive yacht,
Aunt Emily's 'rotten lot'
Turned out to be
The grandest in Durban –
Not half so suburban
As Aunty and me!

Puzzle Poems

Woe-man-gling
Sexual Discrimination Act. International
Women's Year 1975

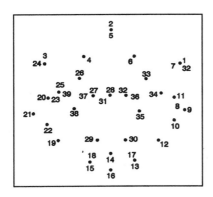

Aunt Dotty

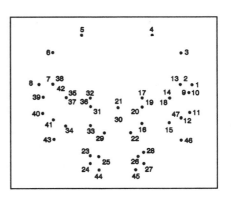

Aunt Dotty's Friend

Join up the dots and solve the
mystery!

Gloomericks

1. Wishful Thinking

A priest in his cassock,
Knelt down on a hassock
To mumble a hymn and a prayer;
But all he could think of
Was quaffing a drink of
Good ale, with a dish of jugged hare, but O
He found that his larder was bare!

Printer's Tempting Offer

If you let me have the priest's address, I'll get my landlady, the widow of Ivor Hunch,
the defunct political forecaster, to send him the *Pope's Nose*! Failing that, she does a
very tempting *Devi*lled Crab with a good pinch of cayenne pepper to bring the flames
from his nostrils! She can also tempt you with a tantalising Frozen Passion Fruit to cool
off with!

2. First Love

Louise, little simpleton!
Went out to Wimbledon
On a late Underground train.
She met a young man there,
Sat on a divan there,
And had to walk home in the rain, poor thing!
But she'll do it all over again!

P.S I never met this delightful Louise. However --- my landlady's *daughter* did more
than she *oughter*. She went off with *Gordon*, an oil-man from *Jordan*. She got very
bored on the stewed lamb and *woughter*! She went across deserts and met a *repoughter*
who whisked her to Paris before Gordon *coughter*. Now, her name is Grace *Auden* and
she lives down in *Morden*, with a son and a *daughter*. Her husband's a *poughter*!

106

Author's Addled Addendum

Then there was sweet Myrtle *Merrivale,* who was chased by a *merry male*, all over *Perivale,* up-down-and-*derry-dale*!

Printer's Regret

And dear Emily *Pugh*, who forgot how to *chew*, and had to drink *dew*! She now lives at *Kew* and married a *Sioux*!

Our Cleaning Lady's Bonus

Don't forget Cecily *Skinner*, who was kidnapped in *Pinner,* but nobody knew how she came home a *sinner*! She was sent up to bed without any *dinner.* Poor Cecily *Skinner!*

Author's Gripe

This is driving me insane! I can't stop thinking of the names of absolutely everyone I know and making up rhymes about them.

P.S. Is there *really* a Sioux still living in Kew? I'd like to meet him.

The Sioux from Kew

107

The (Fifth!) Editor's Choice Cut

Our elusive Author (or Scribbler) is still indisposed. He appears to be wandering through the *terra incognita* of an alcoholic haze. When our Cleaning Lady went round to his Chelsea flat, he was sitting on the floor with his 'peeky-knees', contemplating his *novel*! We are afraid this humour lark has seriously affected his mind. He frightened our good lady by singing some perfectly revolting verses he claims were composed by Julius Caesar on quelling the Saxon pig-breeders:

> *Veni, vidi, vici!*
>
> *I like my bacon streaky!*

This incident was reported recently in The **Pig**-Breeder's Pen Club **Bull**etin.

The Firefly

A firefly flew in at my window
   One sultry summer's night.
I was searching for my slippers,
   So I asked her for a light!

And what d'you think she answered,
   As she glittered like a jewel?
"I can't stay long, my darling one!
   I'm running short of fuel!

Portrait of a Flitter!

Author's Autobiographical Aside

I have to admit that fireflies are *not* terribly attractive close up. They look very much better in the dark – like some humans I know! (Readers of my verses excepted, of course!) And, what's more, they're *fright*fully difficult to sketch as they *will* keep flitting about all the time! (The fireflies, I mean. Not the humans, though they *do* do a fair bit of flitting about as well, if the truth were known!) But these fireflies – really! Flitting here, flitting there, flitting, flitting, flitting! That's all they could do! Pretty useless, don't you think? I saw thousands of them once in a forest during my 'When I was in Bulgaria' days! I remember – how can I forget! – I was chased across a field by a rather boisterous buffalo, fell into an icy pond which I didn't know was there (obviously!) and nearly froze to death. That's what flitting about does for you! The more vulgar Bulgars I was with kept saying silly things like "OOOH!" and "AAAH!" and COR!" Not at me, I hasten to add, covered as I was, from top to bottom, in *rather* smelly buffalo mud. Oh no! They were gawping at the fireflies busily going about their wretched flitting. "OOOH!" "AAAH!" "COR!" they kept saying. All *I* could mutter was "BR-RR!"

Fly-by-nights

> Fireflies only come out at night;
> Some humans stay out late, it's true!
> But human or insect, it's all the same:
> I'm *rather* suspicious of what they do!

Torch Song
Once, I was visited while I slept
By a man with a torch and voluminous bag!
He came through the window and left the same way;
He took all my money and sold all the swag.

The Knew Editor's Exclamation

Give me the animals any day. *They* don't carry torches and swag-bags. At least they do have the decency to come in by the door! That's if they're invited, of course! For goodness' sake, don't let on to the rhinoceros! Especially with *his* party-manners!

Fatal Fable No.6: A Printer's Error
Our sorry (Fifth!) Editor got the *hump*, was told to take a running *jump*! Editing was such a *chore;* he could not bear it any *more*. How many slips he tried to *save* with many a comma and full-*stop*, superfluous phrase to prune and *lop*. With new 'old guard' and old 'new *wave*', he did not know how to *behave*. He dotted i's and crossed the *t's* of many a poet's purple *prose*. Too many hours, was forced to *doze*! He landed with a belly-*flop*, outside our undertaker's *shop*! From desk to churchyard in one *hop*! To grammar, syntax, he was *slave*. Now 'printer's devil' tends his *grave*.

Ladies' Gossip Column

For Hermione Baddeley

"Oh! Oh! Oh!
How nice to see you!"
(Sip! Sip! Sip!)
"And China tea you!"

"Too – too – too
Divine, these cakes, dear!"

"Yes! Yes! Yes!
My husband bakes, dear!"

"You – you – you,
You're born a housewife."

"I – I – I –
I'm such a mouse-wife."

"No! No! No!
You're such a worker.
Scrub! Scrub! Scrub!
You're not a shirker.
Can-can – can
You dance the polka,
Cha-cha-cha
And drink hot vodka?"

"Yes. So-so.
But I'm no slicker.
Slut! Slut! Slut!
To show my nicker!
You – you – you –
You look so chic, dear!
I – I – I –
I feel so bleak, dear."

110

"No! No! No!
You're lovely, charming!
(So-so!) – so – so
So disarming!"
(Mumble-mumble-mumble!)

"Oogh! Did she really?
Well! Well! Well!
Now, what a silly!"

"Pom! Pom! Pom!"
"But did she want to?"
"Rip! Rip! Rip!"

"His tunic off, too?
Wretch! Wretch! Wretch!
It was wrong to! –
Dear! dear! Dear!
But I must go now!"

"Well, bye-bye!
What a blow now!
Do – do – do
Come round again, dear.
(Cackle! Cackle! Cackle!
Just like a hen, dear!)

Going – going – gone!
She looks so solemn
As I scribble, scribble, scribble
For my gossip column.
Oh! Oh! Oh!
She makes me itch!
Slam! Slam! Slam!
SLAM!!!! The bitch!

A Harpy!

The Mating Game

You should always be cautious when entering the zoo:
Animals do things we humans *don't* do!
At least – I don't *think* so, though I have been told
That some of our habits are as old as they're bold!

Our (Sole) Reader's Leery Queery

"Please can you tell me what these habits are?"

Publisher's Rapid Retort

"I'd really rather not say, if you don't mind!"

Stepping out of Line

Birth Sign: A Serious Dilemma

Astraea
refusing to conspire
with mortals, whom she found disgusting
though implicitly trusting
the gods, became a constellation,
a somewhat lonely consolation;
she took the name of Virgo by mistake,
proceeding then to undertake
a life devoid of any sexual factor
and ever since has been
Virgo intacta!

Virgo: "Come up and see me sometime!"   **Venus**: "Don't forget *me* dear!"

Closing Time at The Seven Stars: A Venial Vignette

Poet: I wrote this verse in sign of Virgo, on my natal day.

Virgo: You're feeling sorry for yourself. It's not your fatal day!

Poet: It has not to do with me. I would not deceive you.

Virgo: Ah!   So it has nothing then of you. I could believe you.

Poet: Rest assured, my love does not concern you either!

Virgo: How do you know? It might be, not be, either, neither.

Poet: The words are anyone's. The thought is mine.

Virgo: The theme is not yours alone.. Our love could be divine!

Poet: I want to flee from love's constraints. I am not blind.

Virgo: We women put down roots; you men are like the wind.

Poet: Goodnight, Sweet Lady! I'm safe with feelings from the past.

Virgo: Farewell, then. I'll to my home, the stars. Alone, alas, at last!

Poet: *(Later, I wondered if she thought I thought she wanted love?*
        Or did she think I thought to think to follow her above!)

113

Landlady's Tango

A speck of dust upon the floor!
    No more!
I hadn't time to clean the grate.
    Too late!
She faced me with a steely glare:

    "Beware,
Young man! I've seen enough of life,
    (As wife),
To know you men are all the same.
    Rare game
We women are to your caress,
    And no redress!
You come in late, you singe the mats –
    (And cats)
With dirty dog-ends. And, moreover,
    Casanova!
I've seen you up to tiddly-winks,
    High jinks
With girls who stealthily at night,
    Quite tight!
I've watched them through your keyhole, giggle
    And wriggle
Till I'm beside myself with rage
    To disengage
My eyes. No! No! Not that in *my* house.
    You louse!
Tomorrow, you will pack your bags and go,
    And so
Respectable, that's what my home shall be.
    You'll see.
No more lewd students to bring shame
    On *my* name!"

I did not speak in tones of deep remorse,
       Of course.
I faced her with an angry stare:

       "How dare
You utter calumny and lie,
       You spy!
You landladies are all the same.
       Rare game
We students are to your complaints.
       The saints
Themselves would criticise your right'
       At night,
To lock the bathroom door, and prowl
       And owl
About the corridors to snatch us,
       Catch us
Kissing goodnight up and down the stairs,
       (In pairs).
And I've some news for you – you nasty-minded cat!
       I'm leaving –
Leaving, do you hear? – I've found a flat!"

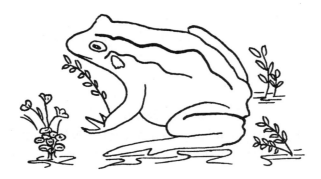

Portrait of a Squatter

115

The Bachelor

O it's lager for Sue and beer for Sal,
Gin for Kate and vodka for Mandy,
Deirdre likes a good Beaujolais,
But I'm looking for a girl to share my shandy.

I'm the man who fancies himself,
A bit of a wag, a bit of a dandy –
The slim-line shirt, the snazzy tie,
And a stock by the bed of chocs and candy.

I'm the man in the crowded bar,
A little too plump, and a little too trendy,
But not half so wet, not nearly so boring,
As that drip in the corner, chatting up Wendy.

I'm the man who is 'over forty',
So available, so handy
For any nice girl who wouldn't mind a chap
That's not too poor and not too randy.

So it's lager with Sue, and beer with Sal,
Gin with Kate and vodka with Mandy,
Deirdre likes a good Beaujolais,
But I'm looking for a girl to share my shandy.

Author's Protest
"This poem is *definitely* about 'a good friend of mine'!
P.S.   He asked me not to mention *all* the girls.

P.P.S.   On second thoughts:

There's Brenda and Mary and Trudie and Dolly
And Sandra and Sarah and Megan and Molly
And Janet and Lizzie and Barbara and Polly
And Hedda and Helga and Hattie and Holly;
There's Caroline, too, but *she* needs some persuasion –
Look! I'll tell you the rest on some other occasion!

P.P.P.S.   None of the above is free on Thursdays. If you know a nice girl who might like a nice chap like 'my friend', ring me up and I'll give you my – er – sorry! *his* telephone number.

Inclined to Drink

The Knew Editor's Roving Report

We have at last been in communication with the missing Author. We tracked him down to the *Cheshire Cheese Tavern*, in a secluded alley off Fleet Street, where we found him slumped in Dr. Johnson's favourite corner, weeping copiously over a large glass of best port. Such is the fate of humorists. In front of him, on the table, were some pathetic verses inspired by the Roman poet Juvenal (no! not Our Centurion!) entitled:

On the Difficulty of Writing Satire

> *"Difficile est satiram scribere"* *
> Why do I feel so cold and fevery?
> Away with the ghosts and all the ghoulery,
> Away with the clowns and all the foolery,
> Away with the louse that spread the rumour
> That I'm going dotty from scribbling humour!

* Juvenal: Sat. 1.30   P.S. Thanks for the tip! I didn't know there was a mount called Juvenal in the 1.30 on Saturday! D'you know if it's Epsom or Newmarket?

How Mistress Hunch came to Harbour a Small Grudge

One day, on coming down the *stairs*, Dame Hunch, slipped up on a pair of *pears,* and fell into the willing *arms*, with much commotion and *alarms*, of inky Printer, Ivor *Grudge.* Now, *he* was not a one to *budge,* nor fall between those sliding *doors* connecting first and second *floors*!

They intend to marry very *soon* – we think the merry month of *June.* Her memory's gone of hubby, Mr. *Hunch*, for now she has another lunch to *munch!* It's not for us to criticise or *judge*, but we hear they plan to have a little *Grudge*!

A Sent-to-Coventry Carol

A Sent-to Coventry Carol

One Sunday, the Organs
And Limbs of the Body
Began to find fault
With Tom, Dick, and Tom Noddy:

"It is we who are blamed,
Over-exercised, lamed;
While Lord Stomach
Relaxes, we stifle!
He sits back to ponder,
Grows fonder and fonder
Of his soufflés
And mousses and trifle."

The notion soon caught on
The more it was thought on,
And soon came the order:
"Go slow in the Works!"
This was on Sunday;
By mid-day on Monday,
The Hands were on strike
With a handful of jerks!

They called it Black Monday,
They downed tools in one day,
Refusing to carry
The food to the Lips.
By Tuesday at breakfast,
The Mouth had to take just
A mouthful of air
In a series of sips.
The last words were uttered,
Were muttered and stuttered

To the Legs as they sought to
Do more than their share.
It was just that they thought to
Do more than they ought to,
Instead of deciding
To stand fair and square.

"Get out! You damned blacklegs!
For every man-jack pegs
His faith in the cause
His hope on the strike.
So down tools and hop it!
This is a closed shop. It
Is just the right day
For a nice country hike."

A Closed Shop

The Teeth joined on Wednesday,
Were drilled in the men's way
To fill in the gap
In the row of events.
"We're clogged up with tartar,
We're playing the martyr.
Our aching self-pity
Must fill in the dents.

"We're not going to chew it.
We're not going to do it.
The food must go rotten,
We refuse to decay.
So let's drop our tackle,
Let's cut out the cackle,
We'll heckle and haggle
At home for the day."

A Public Service

The Throat stopped on Thursday,
Never a worse day
To pander to pride
Or resign from the job,
With the next day as pay-day,
And the chance of a hey-day,
A dance-and-be-gay day
With the Hammersmith mob.

A Pretty Bunch

"O think how I've swallowed
While Lord Stomach has wallowed
In *Champagne Fine Sec*
Or a wine from the Rhine,

123

In *Lobster au Gratin*,
From midnight to *matin*,
Whether breakfast or luncheon
Or asked out to dine.

"With patience I've suffered,
Been badgered and buffered
With hundreds and hundreds
Of swallows a week,
To salve with saliva,
Without a reviver,
A life-time imbibing
And no time to speak!"

Friday – no meeting,
No drinking, no eating.
A gloom now enveloped
The Body at last.
Like bankrupts investing,
Like actors all 'resting',
The Parts of the Body
Resigned to their fast.

On Saturday, unsmiling,
The Body Beguiling
Showed a marked discontentment
At life without food.
A sharpened resentment,
As if it were Lent, meant
A radical change
In the over-all mood!

Stomach grumbled and mumbled,
Legs staggered and stumbled,
But nevertheless
They intended to prove
That they had no compunction,
Continued to function,
Though the Organs grew weary
And did not approve.

Cried the Heart, in elation:
At a Joint consultation:
"Let's try automation
For this how-d'ye-do!"
Thought the Brain: "That invention
Brings only contention;
Why! The idea's insane!
It dispels of man, too!"

The Brain had a brainwave,
Just after the conclave,
To band up together
The Organs and Limbs,
To work in communion,
To form ad trade-union,
With its own special flag
And a few rousing hymns.

"Away with the starvers!
Go, bring on the carvers!
Let's order a banquet;
We've been weak for a week!

We'll open a barrel,
We'll sing an old carol
With a moral to show us
The strength of the meek."

Lord Stomach, in hunger,
Bawled: "I'm not getting younger,
So send down a dish
Or I'll dwindle and die.
I'll give riches and title
If each little bite'll
Bring power to each Part
And add proof to the pie!"

Said the Teeth: "Cut out the cackle!
We're ready to tackle
The whipped cream and trifle
And blackberry tart."
Cried Lord Stomach: "How scrumptious!
So tum-tee-tum-tumptious!
Am receiving you clearly!
Say Grace and let's start."

And thus it all ended
With everything blended
To tickle the Palate
And garnish the vote.
The moral's no swindle:
The Body will dwindle
If the Limbs that shall serve it
Seek to cut their own Throat!

Press Cuttings

This poem is a brilliant exposé of the weakness of the Body-Politic that corrupts from the Inside. — *The Cook's Companion* (Ash Wednesday Edition)

Lord Stomach's predicament is a warning to all those who despise natural foods and idolise the scrumptious! — *The Crude Fude Guide* (Hogmanay Edition)

Conciliation means capitulation! — *United Megaphone* (May Day Edition)
Spinach and a few Capers with Olive Oil is all a man needs. — *Popeye Fan Club*

A Sent-to-Coventry Carol is a masterpiece of ingenuity. Whoever wrote it is a genius of wit and humour. He should be our next Poet Laureate. — *Boilermaker's Beano*

Publisher's Affable Afterthought

These *Sent-to-Coventry* verses Our Author has sent in are a lucky *strike* as the whole country is immobilised. Even though Our Author is rarely Pindaric or *Sapphic*, he is almost invariably *graphic*. These verses first saw the light of day (though with some difficulty as it was night-time!) after a few sundowners sent his head spinning *round* in Cavendish *Square* ('the square circle' mentioned, so the rumour goes, in *The Tortoise and the Turtle*). He was paying one of his Sloane-ranging calls at *The Phoenix*.

A Psychotherapoetical Expert's Probe

Later that night, we tracked our Scribbler down to the snug at the *Three Brewers*, where he was found to be alcoholically *para*lytic. He is a classic case of *para*normal *para*noia of a *para*doxical kind which is difficult to *para*phrase on a *para*graph. I may well be accused, here, of *para*lipsis (or even *para*taxis) but it is *para*mount to draw a *para*llel with Jungian rather than Freudian *para*dox. His humour may be *para*logistic, his wit *para*magnetic, his word-associations born out of a painful process of *para*synthesis. Though it is virtually impossible for us to define the *para*meters of his case, he may, to employ a *para*digm, prove to be a *para*gon of his profession.

A Transcendentalist's Levitated Viewpoint

Our poor suffering Author must seek to rise above the cloudy nothings of this life. He must be persuaded to find comfort in the fact that man's soul is incapable of being *atomised*, as he claims in his Gloomerick, though I hear he gets very *spirited,* and certainly *spirituous*, down at *The Six Bells!* Should he rise to even greater heights of absurdity, he will have to be provided, on the principle of 'pride before the fall!', with a *para*chute!

A Plagiarised Appendix

I'm heartily sick of sick humour!
I'm retiring to somewhere near Woking;
I'm sick of the scandal and rumour;
I'm sick of the punning and joking!

I'm sick of my pulse in the main;
I'm sick of its slowness and quickness;
But I tell you one truth that is plain:
I am heartily sick of all sickness.

Editor's Note: Forgive 'Our Author', Thomas Hood! You wizard of the *word*!
He did not mean to copy you. As rival, he's *absurd*!"

Our (Last) Editor's Final Flip

I have finally decided to cut out this grumbling appendix. It makes the book far too long and is in danger of causing a paper shortage. Now, would you believe it, Our Cleaning Lady has taken to writing her *billets doux* in *verse*, and what is *worse*, leaves them on my desk for *correction* – and ultimately for *collection*! Furthermore, on *reflection*, I need some *protection*! Specially if I mark them: "For *rejection*!"

Scrumptious Verses

Sunday Roast

A Gastronomic Gallop

O for a sizzling, succulent joint!
Bubbling in gravy and cooked to the point:

Roasted on Sunday,
A family-fun day,
With salad on Monday,
A better-than-none day,
Hashed up on Tuesday,
A hard-to-refuse day,
Rissoled on Wednesday,
An ask-in-the-friends day,
Hot again Thursday,
A pinch-on-the-purse day,
Friday's a high-day,
So fish for a Friday,
Oddments on Saturday,
A what-does-it-matter day!

And once more it's Sunday,
A family-fun day,
A fought-well-and-won day,
A better-than-none day,
A hard-to-refuse day,
An out-to-amuse day,
An ask-in-the-friends day,
A first-good-intents day,

A pinch-on-the-purse day,

A nourish-and-nurse day,

O what a high-day!

An eat-well-or-die day,

A what-does-it-matter day,

A bigger-and-fatter day,

O for a sizzling, succulent joint,

Bubbling in gravy and cooked to the point:

    Ad

        in

            fi

                nitum!

Our Cleaning Lady's Conviction

This pome is absolute pawnygraffy to a vedgytarian! I would like to *meat* this 'ere '(Sole) Reader' bleeder! He sounds a bit *fishy* to me! I'm going to tell 'im off about this 'convikshun' biznis. My 'bruvver' is a man with 'convikshuns'. He'd give 'im a good roasting anytime!

Publisher's Butcher's Choice Cut

Why not *jump* off your *rump*, and *purloin* a *sirloin*. You'll soon be on the *mend* with a bit of *best end*.

Publisher's Conviction

I've said all along, Our Scribbler has got a good deal of side and should be hung, drawn and quartered! But then, I *do* have to keep reminding myself that the man is – against all odds – a comic genius!

P. S. Please don't tell him! I'll never hear the last of it. He might even expect to be *paid* for his pains! We *never* pay Our Authors, on principle. They pay *us*! Oh, Vanity!

Tea-Time Recital

For Joyce Grenfell

Author's Perilous Preamble

I was visiting my singing aunt, Celia Spratpuddle, better-known as 'The Nightingale of Neasden'. She invited me to a lamp-shade making day at the local Ladies' Guild near Nine Elms (or was it Seven*oaks*? It certainly wasn't *The Six Bells*!). An elderly writer of verses, a Mr. Joyce, was invited to recite some of his poetical perambulations after tea. As it happened, *Mabel* was quite *able* to organise the *table*, and *Alice*, her friend from Crystal *Palace*, had not a jot of *malice*. But oh dear! Mr. *Joyce* had a feeble *voice* that got woice and woice!

Speaker:	*O Beauteous Stream.................*
Mabel:	............It's best Ceylon!
Speaker:	*I love thee still.............*
Mabel:	...........er – weak or strong?
Speaker:	*Dost thou glide on to distant seas......*
Mabel:	The sandwiches are jam or cheese!
Speaker:	*Alone through forests, undismayed?*
Alice:	I'll take the jam. Is it home-made?
Speaker:	*Thy snowy images of swans......*
Mabel:	Now, how's your cup? *Do* have some scones!
Speaker:	*Cool-mirrored in the silver sheen,*
	Go gracefully, and slowly preen......
Mabel:	Have a cream puff! A little more jam?
	So pleased you came! I really am!
Speaker:	.............*(and slowly preen)*
	Their dainty plumage to the moon.
Mabel:	I think *you* need a *larger* spoon!
Speaker:	*Thou flowest to the ocean's brim......*

Mabel:	More cream, my dear? You're still *quite* slim!
Speaker:	*Eternally, while woodlands mourn*
	The passing day to darkness drawn.
Alice:	Delicious chocolate gâteau, too!
	I *do* love poetry, don't you?

Author's Musical High Note

Celia (neé *Fishpoole*) had something *addishnal*: she could sing like two birds in a *huddle*. She married a *Goldfisch*, a trombonist, a *bold fish*, and called herself Celia Sprat*puddle*! Their life was a terrible *muddle*. But they always made up with a *cuddle,* Mr. Goldfisch and Celia Sprat*puddle*!

Celia Spratpuddle
Shedding her Scales

Our Author's Expiry Notice

Dear Grudge, Please inform the Printer, the Publisher, the Cleaning Lady, the Psychologist (especially the 'Animal' of the species), the Cosmetic Surgeon, Farmer Hodge, the local Vet, the Zoo Keeper, the Cambridge Don, the Knew Editor, and our long-suffering (Sole) Reader, that I shall be giving up comic verse on the advice of my Bank Manager, who has just been short-listed for Poet Laureate. He thinks I might do better writing something more serious. He has probably been in league with Our Cleaning Lady, who is becoming quite conversant with the intricacies of prosody, and has been nominated 'Poet of the Year' by the Cleaning-Ladies Guild. She was awarded the DSO (Domestic Service Order) for her lavatorial prize-winning graffiti art: *Tattoos!*, now on permanent view in the ground-floor Gentleman's toilet at the Town Hall: Monday to Friday 9am to 5 pm. Key available from the resident poet Mrs. Rhoda Bristle-Broome.

P.S. She is entering it for the next Turner Prize (Lavatorial Art Category).

The Chelsea Bunns

A block of flats in Chelsea is but one
Owned by the pastry magnate 'Arfer' Bunn!
Whose daughter Julietta's name befits her,
Especially now she's Giulietta Pizza!
A Sicilian *pasta* mogul is to blame:
He gave her a fortune and a *floury* name!
Her sister, Henrietta, hardly needed dough:
She fled to wicked Paris, where a *beau*
With his *pâtissierie* he wooed and won
The heart (and gold!) of Henrietta Bunn!
Now father 'Arfer' is, alas, no more!
His pastry failed to rise to heights galore!
His Julietta's pasties are 'no go',
And Henrietta really *kneads* the dough!
Her fly Parisian grabbed her cash complete.
The pasta-mogul lives in style in Crete!
If only, of his girls, he could control one,
Old 'Arfer' Bunn would have remained a whole one!

Our Cleaning Lady's Candid Confession

Old 'Arfer' Bunn was a ferret of a *man*! When he appeared, the underworld soon *ran*! Feared by all, he was a cruel *lover*. He was, you see, my muvver's wicked *bruvver*!

P. S.   He made a lot o' *dosh*, mainly by the *cosh*, and ended up quite *posh*!

P.P.S. His nephew, *Henry, ate a bun,* with arsenic as a filling of *refinement*, whilst daughter, *Julie, ate a pizza* mixed with strychnine, and died soon after of a *grave confinement*!

P.P.P.S. Old 'Arfer was disgraced, with shame and *snubs*. I do not know what happened to the *rest*. I've heard they live in comfort in the '*Scrubs*': I'm told it's at Her Majesty's *request*!

Serious Stuff!

At the request of Our Cleaning Lady!

An Eastern Tale

written on waking from a dream on 3ʳᵈ August 1952

A young fakir in a white turban,

seeming not a bit suburban

save for horn-rimmed spectacles western-style,

tried desperately to reconcile

the western and the eastern muse

by a ruse.

In doing so, he lost his concentration,

though by a clever automation

he concealed the fact

that he lacked

sufficient fervour,

was not a just deserver

of the public praise,

which, in his case, deftly allays

the moment of anger

only temporarily; and there is danger

that patience aggravates

(not placates)

an anger, which unassuaged,

contrives to be a caged

monster of the air

with wings of fire

and nostrils breathing flame

to defame

impostors with brimstone –

a grim stone

with which to be bombarded.

His shoes discarded,

the pallid youth, in vain,

(As well as in great and unnecessary pain)

squatted on a bed of nails,

as more experienced fakirs do in Indian tales.

He made no cry of pain

as the stain

of blood crept slowly over the bed,

as he quietly bled.

The restless mob grew gradually irate

as they watched the state

of things proceed.

Indeed,

whereas they first began to laugh

at this pretentious calf,

who dared to show his face

in such a public place,

their laughter turned rapidly to scorn

as the young man grew more and more forlorn,

though he never made a single sound

except the dripping of the blood upon the ground.

His flesh sank deeper and deeper on the nails,

like burning flails

searing the flesh and skin

in expiation of his sin.

A white-haired elder launched a stone,

expertly thrown,

which made a deep incision

on the cheek, a mark of the general derision.

The youth was unperturbed

by this reaction, not at all disturbed

but merely conscious of a clear deficiency

and lack of any real efficiency

to concentrate.

The anger of the crowd did not abate

but grew until the howling mob jeered at the magician

as he squatted there in such a pitiful condition.

Then, suddenly, the Manager appeared,

long-since revered

for his integrity.

He stood before them, pronounced in all solemnity:

"The province of Ambition's throne

is a god of stone!"

In silence then the people cowed

and vowed

never to criticise again,

as wise and holy men,

the actions of the oblique

and weak,

who had not the courage to confess

a deep inner distress

and ancient need

for which they were prepared to bleed.

What's the Use?

For Louis McNeice

Can you see toy castles –
parcels from great-uncles – in the sand,
and buy lollipops for tuppence?

Can you see the out-reached
cold-bleached little hand
of the orphan begging buttons?

Can you see the sumptuous
plumptuous lady with the beard,
and say circuses are fun?

Can you see this earning
ever-turning world in which we're reared
to eat cabbage soup and buns?

Can you see the paste
and waste of wurlitzers and jeans,
and having supper on baked beans?

Can you see it? Can you?

Can you feel your rumbling
grumbling stomach as it turns
and spars with the spaghetti?

Can you feel your ranting
panting heart beat as it burns
on piles of damp confetti?

Can you feel your mounting
founting pulse throb as you scream:
"Age costs me too much to queue"?

Can you feel the rising
sizing need for strawberries and cream,
as the blonde holds out the crutch to you?

Can you feel her groping,
soft-soaping hand grip yours
and your soft heart turns to starch?

Can you feel it? Can you?

Can you hear the munching
crunching bullocks in the field
as they chew at turnip-tops?

Can you hear the shouting
pouting schoolboys' game revealed
as they play at hop-scotch?

Can you hear the vesty
breasty show-girl with Papa,
simpering to seduce the males?

Can you hear the yapping
never-napping beldams in the bar
telling naughty-husband tales?

Can you hear the slinking
plinking of the organ-grinder's sigh
as he makes his monkey cry?

Can you hear it? Can you?

Picture Poem: The Tender Trap!

Our Author's Rapid Recoil

Now! I wonder if this poem 's just *appealing,* or is it just a trifle too *revealing*?
P.S. I'm afraid Megan and Molly and Trudie and Dolly are going to think me a terrible
old cynic! I just pray Barbara and Polly and Hattie and Holly don't see through me. And
what are the wily Mistress Hunch and furtive Master Grudge going to say?

P.P.S. I'm off to find some comfort at *The Rover*, though my friendship with the Man
from Ayr is *over*. You could hardly say I'm sitting here in *clover*! I think I'll give up
verse and be a *rover*. I'll go and catch the next boat-train to *Dover*. I'm really quite a
quiet, reflective *chap*. I'm sure to find some silence at *La Trappe*!

The Income Tax-Collector

If a workman were sure of dreaming every night that he was a king, I believe he would be almost as happy as a king who dreamt every night that he was a workman. – Pascal

Have you ever had the urge
To throw away your old blue serge,
And buy a robe of royal silk,
Wear crown of gold, and bathe in milk,
To satisfy your inner need
To shoot the Star and take the lead?
To get away from kith and kin,
And have your sherbet mixed with gin
Brought on a silver salver by
A sly old Turk with one glass eye,
One watching for the slightest move,
The other blind enough to prove
Your alibi – your need to be
Someone you're not decreed to be?

You sit and ponder and peruse
Some travel agent's brochure, choose
A distant place to get away
From Dick and Flo and Jack and May,
To be a desert-island king
Instead of just an underling
Without a hope of any kind
Of ever being wined and dined
In style on your Director's purse.

This life grows worse for you, and worse.
Then comes that dark and dismal cry:
"Anoint this man, or he will die!"

The crown is placed upon your head –
There are no jewels in a crown of lead! –
Yet life takes on a brighter hue.
You leave the masses for the few.
You smile as subjects kiss your hem
And marvel at your diadem.

Then dream yourself in marbled halls,
Bewailing happiness at walls
Of antique palaces, where dust
Lies thick on power and greed and lust.
You are no desert-island king!
No monarch, no, not anything
Your dreaming led you to believe.
You are a slave! The people grieve.
They criticise you – Right and Left!
Yours is the head whose skull is cleft
By your old trusted Turk, whose eye
Of glass reveals the reason why
You are the Great Dictator now!
Will you, won't you stand and bow?

See how you long to be again
Your former self among the men
Who quietly strive to free themselves
From dull routine, and shelves and shelves
Of dusty files. The longing flies.
The Vision fades. The gruff voice cries:
"Come on! It's time to go. It's time!"
Your heart beats fast as you meekly climb
Down from your throne, only to find
In that unseen light that leads the blind,

Your fear of abdication's gone!
The gilded throne you were sitting on
Was nothing but a leather stool,
Your sceptre just a printer's rule,
The royal robe your old blue serge,
The royal register a splurge
Of figures glumly inked by you
In green and black and red and blue.

The longing fades, the Vision dies,
As out of nowhere someone cries:
"Come, young man! Whatever next!
You work too hard. Find some pretext
To earn yourself a few days off
To take away that hacking cough!"
He smiles the smile of greed and pride,
As you hide those thoughts so hard to hide.
You're not ambitious, just content
To work enough to pay the rent.
You want to be a simple man,
With simple tastes of simple span,
To love the flowers and trees and brooks
Instead of balancing the books!

How can *he* know you're happy here,
With sandwiches and bottled beer!
He interrupts your office lunch:
"You know, young man, I've just a hunch
You'll be no tax-collector.
You'll be, like me, just wait and see,
A Treasury Inspector!"

Time and Space

Our Psychologist's Cure for Lost Marbles

Time and Space

A Mystical Memorandum from Our Author

Look, gaze, or peer into this empty window for as long as you have to, then write down a poem, or draw in to the space whatever you see or imagine there. If you see nothing after an hour, get help quickly! Alternatively, go to bed and DREAM! Then try some more gazing and peering, peering and gazing, and so on.

Warning! – Mind you don't get arrested for loitering!

P.S. The Government hasn't yet thought of a means of taxing our dreams. Please do not suggest it. They'll be taxing my 'peeky-knees', next!

P.P.S. Don't forget to empty your mind before the gazing bit. Of course, if it's empty already, just turn over the page and find out what Our Author saw in *his* window.

P.P.P.S. Now, try again! Remember! This is **SEE-EE- RIOUS STUFF!**

P.P.P.P.S. Don't mention it but we're thinking of entering him for the Turner Prize (Blank Canvas Category).

Picture Poems

Four Reflections

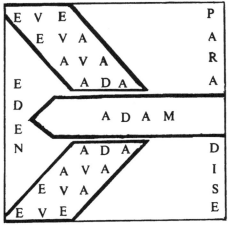

Genesis
or, Space Travel

Eternity
or, A Knotty Problem

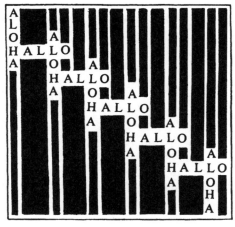

Active Pacifism
or, The Peace of the World

Millennium Star
or, The Year of Our Lord

Author's Last Writes

A Hypochondriac to his G. P.

Prescribe lotions and pills
As a cure for my ills,
And a short sharpish shock for my hiccup;
Some linctus and plasters
(In case of disasters)
And a tonic to give me a peck up.
Dear Doctor, do give me a check-up!

Please tell me, dear Doctor,
Now, can you concoct a
Nice medicine to cure all of these?
I'm so down in the dumps;
Is it measles? Or mumps?
Is it love? – like the birds and the bees?
Or some far more deadly disease?

Is it gout? Is it cancer?
Am I just a romancer?
It is *pain*fully clear I'm in pain!
Is it *quad*ruple *quin*sy?
An attack of the Kinsey?
Do tell me, dear Doctor, again!
Is it housemaid's knee – on the brain?
Do tell me, dear Doctor, again!

Publisher's Pallid Response

Here I am, ladguishigg in bed, with a sore doze add I've had to ask our Pridter to keep thiggs od the boil. I bust 've caught Our Author's co'd. (Sdiff! Sdiff!!)

148

A Loud Report from Our Resident Herbalist

Our Scribbler, in his relentless search for rhymes, has become thoroughly liverish, quiverish and shiverish. He's beginning to *burble,* like a frustrated *gerbel.* He should give himself time off from *rhyme.* He must give up the *verbal* and take up the *herbal*, and sleep on sweet comfort and *thyme*!

Chamber Potty!
Panacea for a Pilloried Poet

He has suffered a Dire Attack! A strong *potion*
He urgently needs, and some camomile *lotion,*
Plus a good dose of senna to give him a *motion!*
Avoid agues and plagues, and domestic *commotion,*
Give him oodles of love, public praise, and *devotion!*
For a hundred years hence, over land, sea and *ocean,*
The world, of his verses, will have not a *notion!*

A Bristler on a Scribbler

Our Author's such a luv'ly *man.* I am his most devoted *fan.*

P.S. Mind you, I don't understand this comedy lark. He's gettin' us all doing it now! He says any twit can write! All you have ter be is a bit of a crackpot. Even the boss has been scribblin' away on the sly, and, as he's at home with a nasty dose of the sick humours, I've cleaned out his drawers – not that I'm nosy, mind! I found an envelope he'd scribbled some lines on.

P.P.S. Our Publisher's followed Our Author's *example.* He has pulled out the *throttle,* drinks wine by the *bottle.* His verse is a pitiful *sample.* I'm not sure it's a leg- or an *arm-pull*!

P.P.P.S. It looks as if he's round the *twist*! I'll be the next on the looney *list.*

149

Soak Song

Purporting to be by our Pickled Publisher

I'm tired and I'm bored,
I'm as drunk as a lord,
I'm muzzy, I'm half-seas over;
I'm whiffled, I'm fuddled,
I'm squiffy, I'm muddled,
And I off for a beer at *The Rover*!

So away with the lot, O
I'm stinko, I'm blotto,
But I'm dashed if I'm going to be mumpish!
I'll be lit up and beery,
I'll be bright-and-good-cheery,
I refuse to be down-in-the-dumpish!

Yet, of all the sad things
This world to us brings,
It's the sadness of making a bloomer!
When you make a poor pun,
It spoils all the fun
And scuttles your sense of humour!

Mrs. Bristle's Dreadful Threat

Funny you should bring *up* about being *down*-in-the-dumpish! I must tell you a.*reelly*
sic[k] dream I'd last night. It made me go all of a shiver and a quiver.

Our Publisher's Selfish Sick Note
written in convalescence
PLEASE don't! Other people's dreamz-zz-zz make me very down-in-the dumpish!

150

Our (Departing!) Editor's Desperate Declaration

Poor Mrs. Bristle had a bit of a down-upsy yesterday and had to go home at lunch-time, suffering from a severe crisis of identity — a fate befalling all of us who have been exposed to Our Author's whimsical follies. The following is an extract from the more coherent parts of her sick note, delivered to me , under cover of darkness, by a weird old man with a beard and dark glasses.

Queer Goings-on in Bethnal Green
or, Round the Bend!

by Rhoda Bristle-Broome, (translated from the Cockney by Ivor Grudge)
2. a.m. by the Cuckoo Clock!

Can you imagine what a shock I had, when I came home from work?
There was a pink scented envelope with the Queen's head on it – all berserk!
Pandemonium! That's what it was! And what's more, under the floor,
There were toadstools two feet high – or well nigh!
Can you imagine the hullabaloo, as I went running to the loo,
To find all the water rushing, as you might say, off to Flushing?
I went down into the kitchen, thinking to put a stitch in
My torn overcoat, and what d'you think I saw, sitting cross-legged on the floor?
An old man with a trailing white beard, drinking up all my brandy! Very handy!
He got up, walked through me like a shiver,
And said: "Oh. well! Time's marching on!" And then he was gone!
I tell you, I don't know what to make of it.
May be it's the flu. Or maybe it's my liver!

Our Publisher's Prostrate Response

Poor dear! She's definitely got more than a bad touch of the sick humours. The old man turned out to be her 'bruvver'[*the one we thought was a rodent*!] on (unofficial) parole from his place of residence at 'The

'My bruvver'!

Scrubs'! He was shaving his head and his grisly black *beard*, and without his dread locks, seemed so dreadfully *weird*. He'd been in a fight and had two black *eyes*, which looked more like a couple of blackcurrant *pies*!

A Humourist's Farewell to Verse

Today, I have finished my humorous verses,
I'm stark staring mad, and what is still worse is
I'm raving, demented, I'm screwy, I'm scatty,
I'm bats in the belfry, I'm addled, I'm batty,
I'm deeply neurotic, I'm downright quixotic,
I'm as mad as a hatter, I'm crazy, psychotic,
I'm a screwball, a crackpot, and worse than all these,
(I hope you don't mention it!) – I talk to the trees!

Printer's Curt Note

I told you so!

From Our Resident Psychologist

Talking to trees is the true sport of *kings*, but by writing good verse you can take to your *wings*. Whether serious or comic, it's so good for your *health*, and if you strike lucky, it might bring you some *wealth*. Success is illusion, and failure *defeats* all the passion and genius that finished poor *Keats*! With lesser pretensions, we can throw down the *die*, and pray that our verse is not cooked in a *pie*!

Decline and Fall: How Our Author Made a Dreadful Discovery

For years I've hoped to find some *firm futurity*, a pair of loving arms, some *warm security*. I set my sights on luscious Mrs. *Hunch*. I sent her posies, roses by the *bunch*. Today I find this Jezebel, Dame *Hunch*, is the self-same one our Printer asked to *lunch*! This fellow, with regret, I now *discover*, had been, the wretch, her sly, long-standing *lover*! I don't begrudge them (undeserved) *goodwill*, though I caught them in cahoots at *Strawberry Hill!* I never saw them on the office *stairs*, nor even caught them kissing *unawares* — unless he donned a cunning, neat *disguise* to hide himself from rival prying *eyes*. And now I find, Dame Hunch has *married Casanova*! It's me should bear the grudge, while they're in *clover*. Which leaves me truly on the shelf -- *kaput!* There's surely been conspiracy *afoot!* I'm all washed up! I think I sense a *tingle* to write some serious stuff, and settle to stay *single*!

Picture Poems

Koobs
or
Upside-down & Back-to-front books

A White Elephant
or
A Vacant Lot!

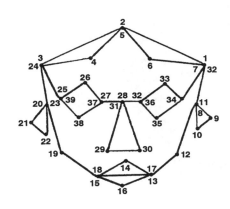

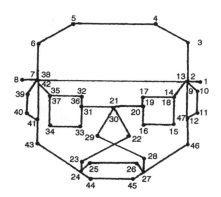

Aunt Dotty Revealed

Aunt Dotty's Friend Unmasked

United at last!

153

Press Cutting: A Guided Tour Through a Linguistic Labyrinth

We hope to organise a series of walking-tours to take in some of the venerable establishments at which our Humourist passed many hapless hours in the composition of such varied comical pieces as *The Rhinoceros, The Octopus, The Butterfly, The Tale of the Querulous Quail, The Firefly, The Bachelor, Tea-Time Recital*, and *A Sent-to-Coventry Carol*.

We intend to set off from *The Six Bells* and proceed by way of *The Queen's Head, The Paxton Arms*, and eventually past, if not into, *The Three Brewers, The Five Bells*, and *The Seven Stars*.

Members of the party may experience some difficulty in keeping up (and possibly upright!) but by licking a finger and holding it up to a south-westerly wind they will be able to follow where their noses lead them, namely that regular final port of call, *The Rovers*. It is regretted that, after a lifetime of 'Words, words, words!', Our Humourist is unable to accompany the tour since he has finally forsaken the spoken word and become a happy Trappist! — *Tippler and Toper's Topographical Guide to London*

The Right-Side-Up Man

What's in a Name?

with a hidden agenda!

A Celebratory Ode to All and Sundry
as reported by Our Publisher in *The Sunday Peep-All*

Draught the First!

It may seem, to the reader, a trifle absurd –
But, on Saturday last, a betrothal occurred –
Between poor *Ivor Grudge* and rich *Ida Hunch* —
The guests, it would seem, were a very mixed bunch!
A military presence was noted by all,
For the service was led by old *Canon Ball*,
The bride wore a dress of fine quilted silk,
A delicious cream colour of rich butter-milk,
Designed by her namesake, soft *Ida Downe*,
A quilt-bedding expert from right out of town.
Her train was acquired from old Montague Burton's
And will serve very well for a pair of net curtains!
Her tiara of violets and freesias just could
Melt a man's heart, or very soon would!
The bouquet, of whitish and purplish bloom,
Was much more in line with a churchyard tomb!
Bridesmaid the First was game *Freda Bird*,
A keen ornithologist, or so I have heard!
Bridesmaid the Second was brave *Eileen Dover*,
Who fell headlong in love with, and glided right over,
A handsome young climber called *'Chalky' Cliff Edge*,
And plumped herself down in a thick prickly hedge!
The Pages assumed a truculent frown,
Little *Ben Dover* and little *Bob Downe*,
Trussed up in tight-fitting blue sailor-suits
(Designed by *Miss Fitt*) were caught in cahoots
With young *Peter Dowt*, a feckless false friend,
Who, of course, came to nothing, I think, in the end.
 The reception was managed by poor *Penny Tent*
Who espoused a *marquis* and lived to repent.
She had tried to elope with loose-living *Guy Ropes,*
Who tricked her and dumped her and dashed all her hopes.
The main toast was given by comic, *Joe King.*
Ivor Koff croaked a poem, then threatened to sing!
Cherry Orchard downed claret, more wine than she oughter,

155

Bruno Ale, a tee-totaller, kept upright on water,
Jay Walker fell into the pool with a splash,
Flo Quickly came in, and went out in a flash,
Gary Baldy was mourning the loss of his toupée,
Which blew off at high speed from his red Austin coupé.
Nora Bone brought her puppy which made a great mess:
It tipped all the trifle right down the bride's dress.

Draught the Second: Notes on some Anecdotal Apologies

Miss *June Marriage* did not, after all, accompany her aunts, *Miss Chance* and *Miss Carriage*. She decided to visit *Miss Match* instead, and give them *both* a miss.

Jerry Bilt was to come with *Iris Kenny-Thynne,* but she accidentally drove her Mercedes into the side of his house, and they both ended up spending the night on the tiles.

Pretty *Rose Erleigh,* late as usual, went to pick up her young farmer friend, *Abel Boddy*, but he slipped up on a fresh cow-pat and fractured his funny-bone. They laughed so much they fell in love and eloped to Paris, where they were classified as foreign Boddy's.

Vera Cross and her brother *Chris Cross* got completely lost when their friends *Wanda Farr* and *Vera Wey* took a wrong turning on the motorway and found themselves in the Lake District.

Count Downe and his nephew *Marcus Downe* became entangled with a pretty young market researcher outside a flower shop, and it took them over an hour to answer five hundred questions on garden pests.

Will Knott and his sister *April May* were to come with *Betty Will,* but, quite surprisingly, *she* wouldn't, so *they* couldn't — and didn't.

Miss Reed was on the point of accepting, but her Belgian cousin, *Kurt Remarque,* insisted on cutting her short.

Sweet *Victoria Spunge* had a bitter argument with her lumpish boy-friend, *Cain Sugar*, who was stuck in a jam and felt very jarred. He sweetened her up by offering her a plum job in his marmalade factory.

When the proceedings were all but over, *Penny Stamp* arrived, arm-in-arm with *Penny Black*, but as expected, they stuck together the whole time.

The Russian visionary baritone, *Ivan Inkling*, and *Sally Vaite*, the dribbling primadonna, who were to have sung a duet from *The Gondoliers*, were cut off by floods when crossing the Fens, and were replaced by excerpts from Handel's *Water Music*.

The famous flea-circus trainer, *Ivan Elavanitch*, was scratched from the entertainment, as was the harpist, that deliciously ticklish *Miss Fidget*, who was indisposed, suffering from a strawberry rash.

P.P.S.   *Anna Rack* was the star — the weather forecaster.
P.S.   *Dick Tate* read the list in his role as toast-master.

Draught the Third!

Among the guests was *General Rumpus*,
And *Roma Lott*, complete with compass!
The General's nephew, *Major Chance*,
Came in on the ferry that morning from France.
But *Francis Farr* and *Frances Deare*
Couldn't afford the champagne and beer.
Then, *Private Bath* and *Lancer Boyle*
Came prancing in with *Penny Royal*.
A rumour spread about the room –
As whispered round by *Rosie Bloom* –
The happy couple gave their thanks
To *Buster Fortune* and *Robin Banks,*
For giving loans to pave the way –
For later Grudges to repay!
The Best Man, *Ivor Bunyan-Payne*,
Gave a lame oration, in the main –
A runner of long-distance fame,
He stumbled on, through name on name,
While *Rhoda Bristle-Broome* was talking
With *Dusty Corner*, up from Dorking.
I left *Neil Lowe*, the social climber,
With *Ivor Punn*, the comic rhymer,
And mildly flirted with *May Knott*,
In the hope she might reveal a lot.
I saw *Gerry Attrick*, retirement-home owner,
With his nurse, *Yootha Nazier*: they called her 'Old *Mona*'.
Vera Preston-Mee, mind, was a thrilling encounter.
Of her many attractions I can only recount her.....

[*this part has been censored by the Lord Chamberlain!*]

The reception is over! I'm ready to drop!
As with all the best verse, I must come to a stop!

The Author's Last Writes

We have received a copy of the following *pro forma* leaked from the office of the Secretary of State for Education. It is especially designed for anthropological, ecological, entomological, eschatological, ethnological, neurological, ornithological, philological, zoological, and even illogical-logical students, both mature and immature, who may ever find themselves sitting for a paper on the dynamics of humour. The special subject is: 'High Brow, or Low Brow?' Answer the following questions in any order you wish but preferably not inside-out or kcab-ot-tnorf! See if you can spot a clue as to the identity of the author.

P.S. Answer only ONE question at a time!

Is this book the work of:

A genius, a madman,
A *thoro*ughly *bad* man,
A talented dunce, or a honey?
A parrot, an ass,
An ape, just as crass,
Or a mastermind worth all your money?
A wit callisthenic,
A sad schizophrenic,
A drunk who's had two for the road?
A crazed paranoic,
A plain man, a stoic,
A fool, or a bumbling toad?

In your opinion, is this koob:

A gross imitation,
A rare revelation,
Is it fun, is it glum and funereal?
Is it matchless, inferior,
Second-rate, or superior,
Is it noble, or low, or ethereal?
Facetious, refined,
Unsurpassed of its kind,
Tests the reader's hard-pressed resilience?
A bizarre tour-de-force,
Or just a lame horse,
Or simply a work of true brilliance?

High Brow?

Or Low Brow?

Publisher's Final Recovery Note

Christmas is coming and, though the goose is not quite as fat as it used to be, we can surely count our mixed blessings! I see a glimmer of hope for Our Author in his last works. He admits to a determination .to be 'bright-and-good-cheery' and, in spite of being jilted by the delightfully seductive Ida Hunch, has at last become 'a right-side-up man'. His legendary self-doubt has been assuaged by the happy outcome of his *check up* with the psychologist, and the even more joyful prospect of a *cheque up* the chimney for him from Santa Claus!

Our Cleaning Lady, Mrs. Bristle-Broome, has put up the decorations in the office, thrown away all the bottles of aspirins, emptied all the ash-trays, wiped away the coffee stains from our desks, decorated Our Author's corner with holly-berries and ivy leaves in the manner of a shrine, and spends her time humming carols as she mops the corridors of power for the last time. I am happy to report that she has recovered her momentary lapse of sanity in the wilds of Bethnal Green. And we hear that Mrs. Ida Grudge has borne a little tiny Grudge!

Now that the book is complete, it is to be hoped that our long-suffering Printer will have his own sense of humour restored to him intact. As for me, my health is 'back to dorbal'!

At last, we can bring down the curtain on Our Author's many characters — those men, women and other beasts who have played their parts so wickedly or amiably in this story. To paraphrase the last lines of *Vanity Fair,* we may close up the box and put the puppets

away, for our play has ended. We can have faith in the notion that, as long as we can go on laughing at ourselves, the world will, most of the time, laugh with us.

Popping up for the last time!

160

The Alphabet Poem

An Epitaph

Picture Poem: a Pocket A to Z

I found me an Atlas to travel the world,
A Bell to foretell my arrival,
A Camel to trammel a desert unfurled,
A Drum to announce my survival,

An Eye to espy the dread dangers ahead,
A Frog to croak songs for the night-time,
A Gate to lead out to the green fields beyond,
A Harp to pluck tunes at the right time,

Green Ivy to dress the old clock in the hall,
Fruit Jelly to wobble and waver,
Plum Jam to sweeten my bittersweet fall
A Jug filled with ale of good flavour,

A Kite to fly up to my dreams in the sky,
A Lamb for its softness, so tender,
A Mite for my time e'er I wither and die,
A Night when the stars shine in splendour,

An Ostrich for plumes to adorn my dear dove,
A Pyramid tomb in the wild wood,
A Palm to wave over my dearest sweet love,
A Quarto of themes from my childhood,

A Quill to write down the great truths of old,
A Rake to retrieve my lost friendships,
A Retort to make age turn to youth, and behold!
A Robin to trill as the sun dips,

A Sabre to battle dark moments of grief,
Bright Saturn to bring me new riches,
A Ship to sail out to the rose coral reef,
A Sock full of toys – not of witches!

A Starfish to point to five ways of my life,
Pale Trail of a snail, shining silver,
An Urn for my ashes, the measure of strife,
A Viper as quick as quicksilver,

A Windmill to turn its white sails on the hill,
An X for my life: *ten* times seven?
A Yew by the church, to remember me still,
And a Zephyr to zigzag to Heaven.

About the Author

Peter Thorogood was educated at Brentwood School, Essex. He studied piano and composition at the Guildhall School of Music and the Royal Irish Academy of Music. After graduating in Modern Languages at Trinity College, Dublin, he taught English in Italy. His popular course on the History of English Literature, at the University of Milan, continued for several years and, on his return to England in 1958, he continued his series of lectures at the British Council in London, with spells as a visiting lecturer in Poland, Israel, Bulgaria and Germany. During this time, he divided his interests between teaching, writing poetry, composing music and researching the life and times of the Victorian poet and caricaturist, Thomas Hood.

In the late 1960's, Peter Thorogood was Radio Talks critic for the BBC periodical, *The Listener,* and compiled a radio series, *English Funny Writing*, for the BBC World Service. In 1967, his translations and elaborations from Federico Garcia Lorca, *The Suite of Mirrors,* were included in a volume of British Council poets. He published two small volumes of poetry, *Love said the Astronomers* (1971) and *The Once-Contented Land* (1972) and, in 1973, an evening of Peter's poetry, music and comic verse was given at Holland House, Kensington, with Alan Wheatley, Joan Murray Simpson and pianist Thalia Myers. Peter's next volume of poems, *Prodigal Son,* came out in 1977.

In 1981 the Oxford Polytechnic Press published his *Thomas Hood and his Relations with the Book trade to 1835,* and in the same year *Thomas Hood's 'Progress of Cant': A Study in Iconography* formed part of a collection of papers published by the Polytechnic of Central London. A programme of Peter Thorogood's poetry, music and comic verse was presented in the Victorian Music Room at his home, St. Mary's House, Bramber, West Sussex, as part of his 60th birthday celebrations in 1987.

Peter Thorogood has devised many recitals of poetry and music, often reading his own poetry and playing his own musical compositions. His programmes have included *A Treasury of Delights* (with Jack May), *The Spirit of Place* (with Matt Wolf), *The Mad, Bad Lord Byron* (with Gwyneth Powell and Alan Leith), *From Beowulf to Virginia Woolf* (with Susan Jameson, Simon Brett, and singer Susan Legg), *Wilde About Oscar* (with Michael Jayston and Rosalind Shanks) and his popular Christmas entertainments, *Wassail!*, *Under the Mistletoe*, and *Christmas Cracker!* Peter's highly successful *The Witty and the Tender Hood* (again with Susan Jameson and Simon Brett) was performed at the Petworth Festival, the National Portrait Gallery, London, and other venues on the occasion of Hood's bi-centenary, and later with musical settings of Hood's poems performed by the Glyndebourne tenor Neil Jenkins with the Brighton Chamber Choir and pianist Terence Allbright. A retrospective selection of Peter Thorogood's poetry and light verse, *In These Places, At These Times*, illustrated with some of his watercolours, was published by the Bramber Press in 1997.